Horace's Hope, Friedman's Folly

Fig. A.1. Public Common Schools: A Promise Tied to Freedom for All Citizens

Horace's Hope, Friedman's Folly

The Purpose and Promise of Public Common Schools in a Democratic Republic

Curtis J. Cardine

ROWMAN & LITTLEFIELD
Lanham • Boulder • New York • London

Published by Rowman & Littlefield
An imprint of The Rowman & Littlefield Publishing Group, Inc.
4501 Forbes Boulevard, Suite 200, Lanham, Maryland 20706
www.rowman.com

86-90 Paul Street, London EC2A 4NE, United Kingdom

Copyright © 2024 by Curtis J. Cardine

All rights reserved. No part of this book may be reproduced in any form or by any electronic or mechanical means, including information storage and retrieval systems, without written permission from the publisher, except by a reviewer who may quote passages in a review.

British Library Cataloguing in Publication Information Available

Library of Congress Cataloging-in-Publication Data

Names: Cardine, Curtis J., 1952– author.
Title: Horace's hope, Friedman's folly : how America sold out its ideals for free public education / Curtis J. Cardine.
Description: Lanham, Maryland : Rowman & Littlefield, 2024. | Includes bibliographical references and index. | Summary: "Horace's Hope, Friedman's Folly explains the forces behind the current efforts to privatize education. It also works to debunk the idea that public education should be based on a capitalistic model of action that places education of our youth into the hands of corporations"— Provided by publisher.
Identifiers: LCCN 2023055684 (print) | LCCN 2023055685 (ebook) | ISBN 9781475872644 (cloth) | ISBN 9781475872651 (paperback) | ISBN 9781475872668 (epub)
Subjects: LCSH: Privatization in education—United States. | Public schools—United States. | Education—Aims and objectives—United States.
Classification: LCC LB2806.36 .C3633 2024 (print) | LCC LB2806.36 (ebook) | DDC 371.010973—dc23/eng/20231218
LC record available at https://lccn.loc.gov/2023055684
LC ebook record available at https://lccn.loc.gov/2023055685

Contents

Introduction	vii
Chapter 1: Schooling Alone: The Resegregation of Our Schools by Color, Ethnicity, and Creed	1
Chapter 2: Local Control of Education Funding and Spending Is Key to Local Control in Public Common Schools in a Republic	15
Chapter 3: "The Public Should No Longer Remain Ignorant"	37
Chapter 4: Horace's Hope and Intent	43
Chapter 5: Paying for Public Common Schools	61
Chapter 6: "That This Education Must Be Nonsectarian"	75
Chapter 7: Why We Have Separation of Church and State	83
Chapter 8: "That Education Should Be Provided by Well-Trained, Professional Teachers"	91
Chapter 9: Restoring Hope to Our Educational Efforts in a Republic	99
Chapter 10: "That This Education Will Be Best Provided in Schools That Embrace Children From a Variety of Backgrounds"	109
Afterword	115
Index	119
About the Author	125

Introduction

> Education is simply the soul of a society as it passes from one generation to another.
>
> —G. K. Chesterton

The United States and the individual states that constitute our union have continuously debated what role, if any, the federal government should play in paying for and providing a tax-funded, common public education system. The question of who should pay for that common public education in a republic and what our obligations and responsibilities to pay for such a public common education should entail were also vigorously and publicly debated prior to the establishment of publicly financed common schools in our republic. What was never in question until the later part of the 20th century was that local control of education was a key factor. Ronald Reagan and Barry Goldwater, icons of conservative thought, both spoke about the need for local control of education. Their positions on federal involvement in education have been twisted by those seeking financial gain by promoting "freedom to choose," a market-based approach to education in our republic.

Horace Mann and the founders knew that in order for a democratic republic to thrive and continue, it would be necessary to provide the financial means for the public to become educated and enlightened citizens of that republic in common, nonsectarian schools. Mann was an American educational reformer who believed that education was the key to moral improvement. He believed that education should be available to all children regardless of their social class or background. This meant making schooling possible for those who could not afford private schools or homeschooling in places like the Dame Schools of his time (the micro-schools of his era). Mann never advocated taking away parents' choice to send their children to private schools. Public common schools would be a tax-funded way to ensure that the republic would pass on its values to all its citizens.

G. K. Chesterton put it succinctly: "Education is simply the soul of a society as it passes from one generation to another." That soul belonged to the society, regardless of the individual members' religion(s). Chesterton, who was a philosopher, was not speaking about Catholic school educations when he wrote this. He was a late convert to Catholicism and wrote this piece while he was still a member of the Anglican Church. The Anglican Church was the Church of England and a part of British public schools. The United States did not want to follow this model in its newly created republic.

Horace Mann's classic *The Republic and the School: Horace Mann on the Education of Free Men* includes a foreword and is edited by America's premier educational historian. That historian, Lawrence A. Cremin, is our starting point for discussing the connection between the purpose and the promise of our public common schools and the success of our republic.

Benjamin Franklin, when asked what form of government we were adopting at the start of our country, replied, "A republic, if you can keep it." Universal public schools were unevenly available in that early republic. The northern states were early adopters, while the South remained locked in a system of private school options paid for by the citizens of the state and unavailable to most citizens and forbidden to slaves. Homeschooling at the time meant bringing a tutor into your mansion or sending your daughter to a Dame School.

Well into the history of public common schools but prior to the requirement to provide a common public education for children in all of our states and territories, a promise was made to the newly freed slaves (and already freed blacks) if they became soldiers in the Union army. Like the "Battle Hymn of the Republic," this promise (see the poster in the figure following the title page) gave the new recruits a cause to fight for.

That promise was made regarding freedom for the slaves and the establishment of public common schools. It was addressed to African American volunteer soldiers when they were recruited to join the Union army in its effort to save our union and abolish slavery. The use of the words "freedom to choose" by Milton Friedman, and echoed by the "choice movement," is an affront to this sacred promise made at the apex of civil division in our country.

The promise was that public common schools would follow victory and emancipation in the newly reunited country. This promise to newly freed slaves was a bold statement since the federal government was not yet involved in public common schools at the time and would not become involved with the financing of those schools until the middle of the 20th century.

The promise wasn't for school choice or vouchers so freemen could go to private schools at the public's expense. That opportunity was there at the time and continues to this day. Private is private, and homeschooling is just that, schooling at home by the parent. That has somehow morphed into expectations for the public to finance these "choices."

We have always been "free to choose." The promise was made to provide common public schools funded by the states and local communities. Horace's hope and intention for our publicly funded common schools was chosen as the method to provide locally controlled public education that would be the choice of all strata of society in our republic.

The first time the federal government became involved in funding public education programs (under the National Defense Education Act of 1958), Arizona's Barry Goldwater famously decried the intrusion of the federal government into what he correctly saw as a function of state and local government. Arizona notably rejected the money allocated to it as a sign of the state's indignation over this federal intrusion into state and local matters.

Things have changed. The federal government is heavily involved in the funding of what is euphemistically termed "freedom to choose," aka "choice." Without tax-free bonds (a state and federal government program), charter schools and private schools would have significant difficulty raising the capital they need to fund their school's construction. Junk bonds and lower-rated bonds, BBB and under, dominate this market.

This higher cost for borrowing is because there are significant financial failure rates in charter and private schools. Additional government involvement in the financing of charters through federal funding via grants for school choice has become the norm, along with state guarantees of charter IDA (Industrial Development Authority) loans. Another federal agency, the U.S. Department of Agriculture (USDA), is involved in funding "choice" buildings in rural areas.

Charters, churches, and public schools took funding from the Paycheck Protection Program (PPP) during the pandemic and the Elementary and Secondary School Emergency Relief (ESSER) fund when those loans became available. In Arizona, 89 out of 229 charter corporations would have finished FY 2020 in the red (with about half of those losses in the millions of dollars) without these additional funds. The figure for FY 2022 included 149 charter corporations out of 234 that would have ended the year with a loss without the government's bailout. This despite the fact that all of the schools collecting these funds kept receiving their share of state funding.

We are investing in "school choices" and facilities with a high failure rate at the expense of our public common schools that have never been "underwater" on their debt. Local control means financial discipline controlled by an elected governing board, not a corporate board.

In most state constitutions, a "free and appropriate" public education or the terms "cherishing education" or "common schools" are components underlying the state's role in educating students in their state.

As the United States expanded and added new states, individual communities set up public common schools as a sign that they were ready to become a part of the fabric and the promise of a democratic republic. Most territories and newly formed states did not wait for action from the territorial or state governments that they were located in before initiating and building their own public common schools. Land for common schools was a part of the process when a territory became a state. Land for schools (common and state colleges) was set aside for that purpose. They did not set up funding for private schools or propose alternatives to public common schools. This was an intentional act.

This book is dedicated to providing the background information regarding the establishment of public common schools in our country and the founders' reasoning about what a public common education should entail. It is a counterpoint to those who advocate for privatization and profiteering from the funds we have committed to education. Public education for our republic, if we can keep it.

The purpose and promise of that publicly paid for education in our republic is what is termed "Horace's Hope." There is still hope for that to continue to benefit all our citizens in the future if we act to ensure that privatization of public education is contained. We, the people, need to act like we are citizens of that republic Franklin spoke about.

Chapter 1

Schooling Alone

The Resegregation of Our Schools by Color, Ethnicity, and Creed

One of the Massachusetts Board of Education's purposes in seeking to establish a normal school at Salem, Massachusetts, in 1854 was to place a teachers' preparation program (normal school) in a city that had always provided an integrated public education to its citizens. This planned integration was in large part due to the amount of freemen who were part of the city's large maritime workforce. At the time, Salem was the premier port in the United States.[1]

The establishment of Salem Normal School took place while Horace Mann was still alive but after he had left Massachusetts to establish Antioch College (an integrated college that followed Oberlin College in admitting women to its student ranks) in Ohio. Salem Normal School did not originally accept male applicants, thus establishing a means for females to lead the way in the teaching profession. The board of education in Massachusetts changed this "females only" policy in 1898. Salem State's addition of a commercial program in 1908 was when the school's population spiked. Salem was the fourth normal school in Massachusetts and the tenth in the United States.

Salem Normal School's most notable graduate at the time was Charlotte Forten, the first African American graduate of a normal school.[2] Ms. Forten was the granddaughter of Revolutionary War hero and American entrepreneur James Forten[3] of Philadelphia, a key advocate for public education in that city. As noted in Salem Normal School's history,

> Salem Normal School alumnae took community service well beyond Massachusetts' borders. Charlotte Forten, the school's first African American student and a graduate of the class of 1856, was the first northern African American school teacher to journey south to teach freed slaves. Other graduates

from Salem would disburse to teach in elementary and high schools as far afield as Africa, the Middle East and Asia. As the demand for teachers increased nationwide, Salem Normal School prospered.

The school is now called the University of Massachusetts at Salem. While attending school there as an undergraduate from 1970 to 1974, the author had the chance to review firsthand accounts of the early years of Salem State and to begin to appreciate the role Horace Mann had in our public common schools origins. This early inclusion of black educators in teacher preparation programs was just one of the reasons that Horace Mann's detractors and anti–public school forces had for rejecting the premises of a common public education. This and opposition from churches to schools that they did not control made up the "conservative" side of the debates regarding the establishment of common schools at this juncture in American history. These fights have continued into the present day.

CHOICE AND VOUCHERS AS A POLITICAL REBUTTAL TO *BROWN V. BOARD OF EDUCATION*

As a counterpoint to Friedman's economic theories regarding public education, the Institute for New Economic Thinking[4] published Nancy MacLean's working paper "How Milton Friedman Exploited White Supremacy to Privatize Education." This illustrated how the *Brown v. Board of Education* ruling became a rallying point for the goal of libertarians to make educating children the parents' responsibility, not the "government's." This also meant that parents would ultimately pay for that education.

> Perhaps most tellingly, though, the ultimate purpose was not really to benefit parents and children, even the white ones who patronized the new segregation academies. For Friedman and the libertarians, school choice was and is a strategy to ultimately offload the burden of paying for education onto parents, thus harming the educational prospects of most youth. As we will see, Friedman himself hoped it would discourage low-income parents from having children in a form of economic social engineering reminiscent of eugenics. He predicted that once they had to pay the entire cost of schooling from their own earnings, they would make different reproductive decisions.[5]

That last line is telling. Birth control via educational cost decisions made by "enlightened" parents.

The move to make the transition to a model where parents paid for education required clarifying first that education is a state issue rather than a local matter. The effort to base the transition on an economic theory (capitalism) and promises of "freedom to choose" had its roots, or so the theorists believed, in the Tenth Amendment to the Constitution.

THE TENTH AMENDMENT

The powers not delegated to the United States by the Constitution, nor prohibited by it to the states, are reserved to the states respectively, or to the people. (Amendment X to the U.S. Constitution)

Similar to the way that "conservatives" tout the Second Amendment while leaving out the entire context of the phrase, "A well-regulated Militia, being necessary to the security of a Free State, the right of the people to keep and bear Arms, shall not be infringed,"[6] neoconservatives and libertarians tend to ignore the Tenth Amendment's last four words, "or to the people," which the writers of the Constitution meant as locally elected governing bodies in a democratic republic, that is, representative democracy and private citizens organizing to petition the government. Public education was founded on local control, not state and federal legislative decisions to undermine that local control and sell out to private interests.

Most of the efforts to provide educational choice paid for by taxpayer funds assert that it is the state's right to do so by using new regulations and rules created by federal and state legislation. These governments willfully ignore or minimize the fact that local school districts are controlled by elected boards. As elected officials, school boards are the representatives of the people regarding public education at the local level. The public also owns the means (i.e., buildings and property) to provide that education. This control means that the local owners can decide what kind of debt they can afford or will allow for educational facilities, which is why we vote on bond issues during an election cycle. Charters and private schools use private equity firms and sometimes banks and other meta-charter groups that provide funding "services" for this purpose. They are not under the same financial constraints as districts. They can assume debt beyond their means to pay for it. The use of "projections" of student growth is part of these financial deals, as are delayed (up to two years) payments of debt and interest-only payments. These are the same financial tools that were used prior to the last real estate market crash and bank failures in 1999 continuing into 2000.

The federal government had to step in with a bailout of these firms.

State Versus Local Control

In recent times, several of our states have taken the will of the people, as expressed in petitioned articles in the individual states, out of their legislative decision making on educational funding. These state legislators regard it as their right as legislators to make rule changes regarding providing a public education and the use of the state's portion of educational funding. Similar moves to curtail local communities from establishing ordinances that the state does not agree with (e.g., banning the use of plastic bags in the town) have been common.

An oft-heard justification for this stance is that "we, the state representatives, have been chosen to represent the people." They have assumed that it is their prerogative under the Tenth Amendment and the state constitution to legislate "choice" and vouchers into existence.

FIRST AMENDMENT RIGHTS

This ignoring of the public's will should set off alarms for those favoring "choice" as well as for those who are against it. This mind-set constitutes a total disregard for and minimization of the First Amendment's right of citizens to petition the government. This fundamental right has been assailed and limited by those attempting to push forward the "right to choose." This from legislatures that don't find it troublesome that they can take legislative actions to ban citizens' right to choose to petition their government by erecting obstacles and arcane rules for collecting petition signatures. It is easy to guess how these same legislators rule on women's right to choose for their own bodies and lifestyles.

Ignoring the Will of the People

An example from Arizona in FY 2022 is used to illustrate this phenomenon. Even when a supermajority of voters (>60% of the vote) voted to limit vouchers, state lawmakers pushed through a universal voucher expansion. The most recent example is the Arizona legislature's expansion of vouchers (AKA "Scholarships") to all school-aged children in the state.[7]

Packing the Supreme Court

The loading of the federal and state supreme courts with "conservative" justices has led to a series of recent decisions that have taken the separation clause and antidiscrimination rules to ludicrous interpretations, including the recent ruling favoring sectarian education as a "choice" for parents when the state pays tuition costs to a parent as reimbursement for the cost to the parent of a private school. This ruling defies the choice made by the people of those communities, mostly in New England states like Maine, when they have to forgo building their own public high school and being able to send their students to a local nonsectarian private school.

The processes used by the Senate and House of Representatives to block President Obama's ability to put forward a candidate at the end of his term tell a tale. This same process was used to allow President Trump to nominate and get confirmed his choice for Supreme Court in his last days in office.

It is clear in the data on private placement that the majority of funding has gone to sectarian schools. What may alarm advocates of these programs is that most of the identified uses of the new universal voucher programs either were in the prior school tuition organization (STO) programs, or they were paying for their own private educations.

This has created a new cost to the state that will most likely hit $900 million in FY 2024.

Clearly the lion's share of these public dollars are going to religious "choices" of the parents, not nonsectarian schools. Vouchers have the same track record in states that have experimented with them. The other thing that is clear is that most of these parents were already paying for their child's education themselves, a stated long-term libertarian goal, prior to those parents accepting vouchers. Be careful what "choices" you wish for; your children and grandchildren will pay the price in the future when true capitalism takes

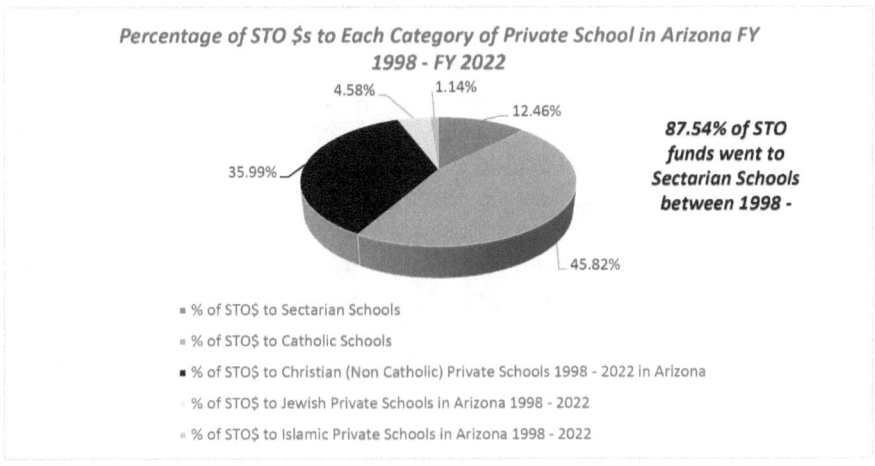

Figure 1.1. Distribution of Student Tuition Organization Funds Since FY 1998
Source: Arizona Department of Revenue report for FY 2022 on STOs, collated by Grand Canyon Institute.

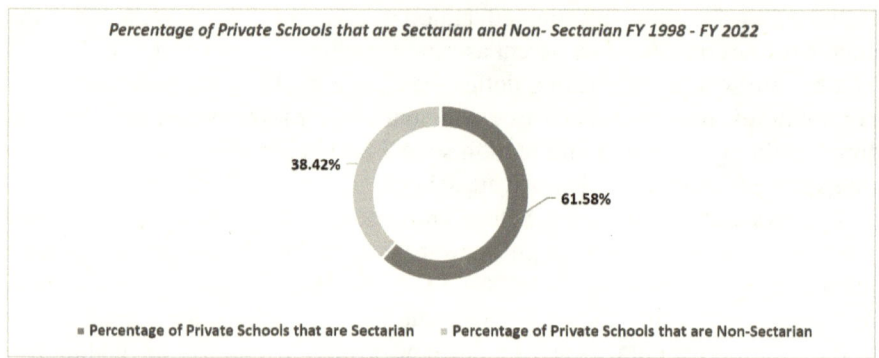

Figure 1.2. Percentage of Private Schools That Are Sectarian and Nonsectarian
Source: Arizona Department of Revenue report for FY 2022 on STOs, collated by Grand Canyon Institute.

place and market education returns to our country. Parents pay for all of their choices.

AN ONGOING DEBATE

The debate regarding the need for and financing of public education and who should be eligible for taxpayer funds for a public education has raged since the beginning of the republic.

The separation of church and state, which is in the Constitution (see the establishment clause[8]), was always a major consideration and a component part of a free and appropriate education funded by taxpayer dollars. This in spite of efforts by the major religions of the time to make education a function of the Christian churches that existed at that time that were anxious to check the growing power of the Catholic schools in those parishes. Churches at the time argued that ministers' salaries should also be borne by the local community. Of course, which ministers would be compensated would be up to the town fathers. None of these efforts to infuse religion into our public spaces passed at the time. The repetition of the phrase "at the time" in this paragraph is deliberate.

Church preferences in this country have always been a changing component of our populations. Animosities toward Jews, Catholics, LDS (Mormons), and Muslims have always existed. We are not a "Christian nationalist" country, although the leaders of choice efforts would like you to believe that is true. We are a democratic republic.

RELIGIOUS DISCRIMINATION BY THE PUBLIC COMMON SCHOOLS WAS SWIFTLY ENDED

When the Lowell Public Schools tried to discriminate against hiring a Catholic teacher, the state board of education made clear that this was a violation of the hiring rules and was unfairly based on the religious prejudice of the Lowell Public School's board of education. The board did not defend this policy due to the First Amendment rights of teachers and the fact that having to state your religion on an application was considered unlawful.

In contrast, churches that run private schools can and do discriminate based on the faith of those applying to teach at their schools. In cases where the church needs to make an emergency hire (i.e., no qualified members of their faith apply), they compel the non–church member to make a pledge not to say anything that could be construed as going against the church's teachings. This practice is protected, as the Supreme Court has declared that it is the right of a religious group to discriminate against individuals based on the organization's religious beliefs. That is, a Christian school in Arizona would not allow a child with two gay men as her parents to attend their school.

A public, common education as articulated by Horace Mann was designed to benefit the common citizen and the republic. He, and the founders, believed that government by the people and for the people needed a common education, free of sectarian influences and religious indoctrination,[9] one that would ensure that all the people in our republic had the capacity, opportunity, and ability to participate fully in our democratic republic.[10]

The founders knew that education was important to the success of the republic.

> The Founding Fathers maintained that the success of the fragile American democracy would depend on the competency of its citizens. They believed strongly that preserving democracy would require an educated population that could understand political and social issues and would participate in civic life, vote wisely, protect their rights and freedoms, and resist tyrants and demagogues.
>
> Character and virtue were also considered essential to good citizenship, and education was seen as a means to provide moral instruction and build character. While voters were limited to white males, many leaders of the early nation also supported educating girls on the grounds that mothers were responsible for educating their own children, were partners on family farms, and set a tone for the virtues of the nation. The nation's founders recognized that educating people for citizenship would be difficult to accomplish without a more systematic approach to schooling. Soon after the American Revolution, Thomas Jefferson, John Adams, and other early leaders proposed the creation of a more formal and unified system of publicly funded schools. While some Northeastern communities had already established publicly funded or free schools by the late 1780s,

the concept of free public education did not begin to take hold on a wider scale until the 1830s.[11]

Universal public education was not established in all the states until the 1920s. The prior year (1919), the states had started eliminating child labor throughout the United States via child labor laws. The first national child labor law came during the second term of Franklin Roosevelt (the Fair Labor Standards Act of 1938).[12]

The founders did provide legislative mechanisms to ensure that education would be a vital and viable part of the republic's growth. This clear desire for a free, publicly paid for common education is contained within the two Northwest Ordinance articles that provided land set-asides for public education in all territories seeking to become states in every county of the new state.

The intent was to encourage education, not require it, by providing for land set aside specifically for this purpose. Public education in the republic was never meant or designed to be an entitlement. You could choose to educate your child by electing to send them to private schools at your own expense or to attend sectarian schools, again at your own expense. Public education was instituted to provide an equal opportunity for all citizens to achieve a basic common education that taught them how to be productive participating citizens in our democratic republic. The Northwest Ordinances also forbid the northwestern territories from entering as slave states and banned slavery within those territories.

The Northwest Ordinances also stated that religion is a key component of what is necessary for good government. These ordinances preceded the Constitution and the founders' clearly stated desire in that document to protect freedom of religion while keeping a firm wall of separation between church and state.

> Religion, morality and knowledge, being necessary to good government and the happiness of mankind, schools and the means of education shall forever be encouraged. (Article III of the Northwest Ordinance of 1787)

As noted, the Northwest Ordinance(s) also forbid slavery in the states entering the union under its auspices, a component of those ordinances that was opposed by delegates to the Continental Congress from the South.

The Wall of Separation

The "wall of separation" is an oft-quoted yet infrequently understood phrase regarding church and state relationships. The phrase is attributed to Thomas Jefferson. Jefferson noted that the "wall of separation" was designed to protect freedom of religion and keep the government out of favoring one religion over another, either by establishing a religion or by financing one through public means. Jefferson made this clear in his letter to the Danbury Baptist Church in Connecticut.

Gentlemen

The affectionate sentiments of esteem and approbation which you are so good as to express towards me, on behalf of the Danbury Baptist association, give me the highest satisfaction. My duties dictate a faithful and zealous pursuit of the interests of my constituents, & in proportion as they are persuaded of my fidelity to those duties, the discharge of them becomes more and more pleasing.

Believing with you that religion is a matter which lies solely between Man & his God, that he owes account to none other for his faith or his worship, that the legitimate powers of government reach actions only, & not opinions, I contemplate with sovereign reverence that act of the whole American people which declared that their legislature should "make no law respecting an establishment of religion, or prohibiting the free exercise thereof," thus building a wall of separation between Church & State. Adhering to this expression of the supreme will of the nation in behalf of the rights of conscience, I shall see with sincere satisfaction the progress of those sentiments which tend to restore to man all his natural rights, convinced he has no natural right in opposition to his social duties.

I reciprocate your kind prayers for the protection & blessing of the common father and creator of man, and tender you for yourselves & your religious association, assurances of my high respect & esteem.[13]

Thomas Jefferson

Jan. 1. 1802

PUBLIC VERSUS PRIVATE PROPERTIES

Public common school properties are held in common by the citizens of the state and the district they are located in. In many New England towns, the land used for public schools was donated by a local farmer for the express purpose of building a public school.

Private charters and private schools (sectarian and nonsectarian) are not held in common. They are private properties.

Churches and their church-owned properties (e.g., schools) are typically exempt from property taxes. Those taxes are the primary revenue source for our common public schools. The same tax rules are true for privately held nonprofit charter school properties. Any use of public funding for church-owned educational facilities and profit-generating activities at those facilities beg the question of why these institutions should still be exempt from property taxes.

Arizona law on this tax exemption is typical.

> Property or buildings that are used or held primarily for religious worship, including land, improvements, furniture and equipment, are exempt from taxation if the property is not used or held for profit. (A.R.S. 42–11109(A).ex)

Charter school exemption from these taxes in Arizona is also typical in states with charter schools.

> Property and buildings, including land, improvements, furniture and equipment, that are owned by a nonprofit organization that is recognized under section 501(c) (3) of the internal revenue code and that operates as:
>
> 1. A charter school pursuant to section 15–183 are exempt from taxation beginning on the date the nonprofit organization acquires ownership of the property and buildings if the property and buildings are used for education and are not used or held for profit. (A.R.S. 421104 (C 1))

Private sectarian and nonsectarian schools are designed to make money for those businesses whether they be religious in nature or not. Any business knows that the three most important business considerations are location, location, and location.

As state legislatures have loosened the rules regarding the use of public funds for private and sectarian schools, we have de facto eliminated the need to keep these properties off the tax rolls. It is obvious that these properties are held for profit.

When the properties are sold, there are often millions made on the sale by the prior owner of the charter. Churches routinely sell off unused properties and parcels of land. The wall that Jefferson spoke of protecting those churches has been torn down by those seeking to offer "choice" paid for by taxpayer funds. The natural consequences of removing the wall begs these questions:

- Why should the users of tax-generated funds to pay for education properties their organizations own be tax exempt from the primary source (property taxes) for funding public common schools?
- Why should the prime users of tax-free junk bonds, pushed by Wall Street hedge fund managers, get the added benefit of tax-exempt bond funding?

- There is no benefit to the general public from real estate transactions involving charter schools and private schools. Fortunes have been made by selling those assets when the owners of those properties decide to "sell" their charter or private school.
- This is especially true when the school goes from being a "for-profit" to a nonprofit operation. The original owners cash out their property investments when the new nonprofit buys out those assets. This results in a high debt-to-asset ratio for the new buyer.
- How do we, the public, recover our investment in these properties? The public does not realize any gain from its misdirected largesse. Wall Street investors are the beneficiaries of billions of dollars in interest payments on properties that are overleveraged. The public has no stake in those properties.
- Why do IDA loan payments get paid directly from state department of education funds first, before the money for educating the students is sent to the receiving charter? This process is known as an intercept.
- Why are we guaranteeing new debt for charters who qualify for guaranteed construction funding from the federal and state government?
  - Guaranteed loans for properties we do not own. The Department of Education created federal and state guaranteed loan programs for privately held educational facilities in FY 2017 under the leadership of Betsy DeVos. The public is now "on the hook" for those guaranteed loans being repaid to private equity bondholders.

SEPARATE AND UNEQUAL

We ask this question: By funding a "choice" that allows us to resegregate by religion, economic class, gender, sexual identity, and in many cases political persuasion, are we not sidestepping the fact that "separate but equal" is not "equal"? Legislation allowing for the use of state funding for private placements specifically lacks the rigor of the equal employment opportunity requirements, allowing the private school to discriminate in its hiring and student-selection processes.

Bypassing Federal Handicap Laws

Schooling at separate private placements paid for by public funding is leading us to a place where we will no longer have a community-owned school in common where all citizens are welcome. The Education for All Handicapped Children Act (Public Law 94–142) was specifically geared to the prejudice against handicapped children and cited the Americans with Disabilities Act as one of its justifications. A tax-funded method of providing education for our children is in the interest of the republic. That interest, and the justification for the use of tax funds from state and local sources, is the cornerstone of what constitutes a publicly funded common education. This was Horace Mann's intention for public common schools in a democratic republic (Mann, 1957).

The founders' and Horace's hopes for a free and common education in our republic paid for and governed locally are being usurped by efforts to:

- Treat public education as an entitlement to state and federal government financing of your choice. Efforts to tap into local funding for these private projects are underway.
- Use those funds to subsidize and pay for sectarian and nonsectarian private educations. The issue: sectarian educations are embedded with indoctrination into the doctrines underlying the religious sects running those private schools.[14]
- Eventually make all education a private matter, with parents holding full liability for its cost.

Chapter 10 discusses this topic and defines what Horace Mann meant when his stated, "That this education will be best provided in schools that embrace children from a variety of backgrounds."

NOTES

1. This preeminence as a port ended with the introduction of clipper ships, which had a larger draft than Salem harbor could accommodate (30 feet). Boston eclipsed Salem as a port for clipper ships. Salem's thriving port became obsolete.

2. https://www.salemstate.edu/salem-state-difference/facts-and-figures/university-history

3. https://www.amrevmuseum.org/exhibits/black-founders-the-forten-family-of-philadelphia

4. https://www.ineteconomics.org/research/research-papers/how-milton-friedman-exploited-white-supremacy-to-privatize-education

5. As Robert W. Poole of the Reason Foundation once put it, the libertarian dream is a "full liability society." That is, you make the choice to have children? Fine, but do not expect other taxpayers to help you in any way. It was your choice, and now you bear full liability for all its costs. Robert W. Poole Jr., "Reason and Ecology," in *Outside, Looking In: Critiques of American Policies and Institutions, Left and Right* (New York: Harper & Row, 1972), 253. Cited from https://www.ineteconomics.org/uploads/papers/WP_161-MacLean.pdf

6. https://constitutioncenter.org/images/uploads/news/CNN_Aug_11.pdf

7. https://azcapitoltimes.com/news/2023/02/06/nation-watches-as-arizonas-universal-esa-voucher-fiasco-fails

8. https://www.uscourts.gov/educational-resources/educational-activities/first-amendment-and-religion

9. One of the current rallying cries of the forces pushing for choice is that public "government" schools are indoctrinating our children with "woke" ideas. They ignore the fact that the private religious schools now include Catholic, Eastern Orthodox, Protestant (nondenominational Christian), Lutheran, Baptist, Anglican (Church of England), Islamic, and Jewish schools, along with Mystic Native entities in Arizona. For a complete list along with amounts taken in FY 2022, go to www.grandcanyoninstitute.org.

10. The "Olde Deluder Satan" law that pre-dated the American Revolution was specifically for giving children enough of an education, at public expense, that would allow them to read the Bible, and avoid temptation. The Horn Books of the times featured the Lord's Prayer (the Protestant version) and the alphabet. The idea was to create an education for the Puritans that gave children the tools to not be deluded by Satan. Again, this pre-dated the U.S. Constitution.

11. See https://files.eric.ed.gov/fulltext/ED606970.pdf

12. https://laborcenter.uiowa.edu/special-projects/child-labor-public-education-project/about-child-labor/child-labor-us-history

13. See https://www.loc.gov/loc/lcib/9806/danpre.html

14. Any graduate of Catholic school, such as the author, will easily recite the Apostle's Creed (aka the Nicene Creed), which lays claim to the superiority of Catholicism over all other religions. A copy is available here: https://www.knightsoftheholyeucharist.com/wp-content/uploads/2019/01/Apostles-Creed.pdf. Protestant faiths have their own version of this creed.

REFERENCE

Mann, H. (1957). *The republic and the school: The education of free men.* New York: Teachers College, Columbia University.

Chapter 2

Local Control of Education Funding and Spending Is Key to Local Control in Public Common Schools in a Republic

MARKET ECONOMICS AND PRIVATE OWNERSHIP OF PUBLIC ASSETS WERE NEVER PART OF THE GOALS FOR PUBLIC COMMON SCHOOLS

The clearest delineator regarding why paying for private school tuitions is not the intent or a purpose for a republican form of government providing a public common education is that the property and the governance of these "choices" is controlled by corporate owners (and in most cases with private schools, sectarian organizations, i.e., religious sects). We are indirectly providing funding for private organizations to purchase land and buildings and losing control of those physical assets in the process. Private and corporately owned charter schools are not common school properties that are held in common by the people.

Once this type of payment for parental choices from the state became available, history shows that the private schools raise their tuition expecting that now the parents can afford to pay more of their own money for their child's private education. Charters also receive a full share of state funding for education without regard for equalization formulas designed to equalize the state's contributions to different school districts.

It's About the Money

When the promoters of school choice say, "It's not about the money," it's about the money.

Private charter management group owners routinely take multimillion-dollar distributions on their management group's profits and from the sale of buildings and intellectual properties owned by the group. Related party transactions are the norm. Revenues spent at private schools indirectly benefit the owners and directors of those private schools' financial interests. This is especially true in schools with over 1,500 students. Organized religions that operate "private" schools use their profits to benefit the religious organization they are affiliated with.

Following the Money

In open markets, one can expect that monopolies will develop and corporate takeovers will occur. As this market-based educational environment matures, there is a consistent and constant acquisition of our charter and private school management groups, including by private equity firms in China (in the for-profit space) and other players in the international equity game. Capturing a "name brand" is the goal of these firms.

Market Consolidation

One of the known dangers of unbridled free market capitalism is the creation of monopolies and price fixing by those monopolies. The payments of lobbying groups devoted to influencing legislatures to provide more and more funding to these organizations is recorded in the firm's audits and in the IRS 990 reporting for nonprofits. Advertising expenses often run into the millions of dollars for large online schools. Churches advertise during their services to a captive audience.

The major players in charter schools are controlling larger and larger shares of our state funding for "public education." These nonprofit charter groups are often controlled by for-profit management corporations. These firms then become targets for equity funds and takeovers of their private schools and management groups by international groups backed by foreign and domestic investors.

The consolidation of the charter market is illustrated in Arizona, a state where charters have existed since 1994.

The dangers of this type of corporate takeover of private schools by private equity firms are the topic of a recent article in *Education Next*.[1] Key in this article are the concerns of the parents about these private schools. The parents

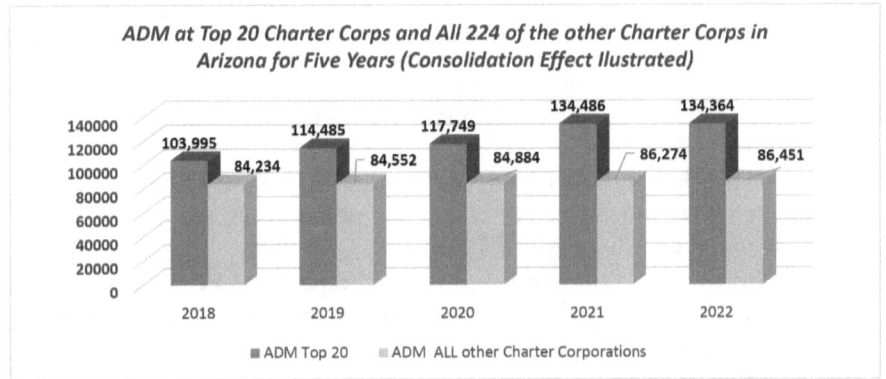

Figure 2.1. Consolidation of the Charter Market in Arizona, FY 2018–FY 2022
Source: Arizona Department of Education annual financial reports (AFRs) data on average daily membership (ADM), collated by the author.

were not consulted about the sale, nor did they have the right to be, as it concerned a private for-profit corporation.

> Last month, BASIS Independent Schools was sold to a company backed by a China-based investment firm. (The sale does not affect the charter schools.) Leslie Brody of the *Wall Street Journal* reports that families at the private BASIS Independent School in New York City have written a letter to the company expressing concern about what this sale will mean for their school.
> Some parents are worried that BASIS private schools will no longer be so closely connected to the high-performing BASIS charter schools. Other parents are worried about the fact that the sale involves China. According to Brody, one New York City parent said the purchase of the school by a group backed by Chinese investors raised questions about privacy of children's personal data. "What does that mean for our kids' school records and medical records?" she asked. "Will they follow the rules?"

Do Private Equity Funds or the Chinese Ever Follow the Rules?

This is not the first case of Chinese investors buying private K–12 schools in the United States. The group that purchased BASIS Independent Schools (not BASIS Charter Group) now controls more than 238 schools with 41,000 students, Brody reports. The schools are located in 18 states. Last year, the group, called Spring Education Group, purchased Nobel Learning.

Nobel Learning Communities Inc. operates a network of for-profit private schools that include preschools, elementary schools, middle schools, and specialty high schools. (Most private schools are nonprofits.) The company also provides various supplemental educational services, including before- and after-school programs, a summer program, learning support programs, and camps. ClassWallet, a program used to authorize and pay "vouchers," winds up approving charges to these groups. Preschools and day care are big business in this county, and often the home corporation is located outside the United States.

Before it purchased Nobel Learning, Spring Education Group purchased Stratford Schools, which operates for-profit private preschools, elementary schools, and middle schools in California.

Spring Education Group is a portfolio company of Primavera Capital Group. According to its website, Primavera Capital Group is a China-based global investment firm that manages funds "for leading institutions, corporations, and families in China and around the world." Primavera claims on their webpage that they are "investing where the future is." That future is not consistent with the promises of public education in a republic. That future is also not consistent with the establishment clause of the Constitution when those "private" schools are affiliated with a religious sect. We are funding private educations that indoctrinate children in the tenets of the religion controlling the school.

One of the complaints promulgated by the "choice" industry regarding our public schools is that they are indoctrinating our children with a liberal bent on our country's history. Turning Point USA, run by Charlie Kirk, is one of the chief proponents of this false narrative. What these organizations fail to mention is that sectarian organizations by their very nature seek to teach the tenets of their church as part of their educational program. They are, after all, the educational arms of the churches they represent, with clear lines as to who is in charge of these schools.

The choice of a religious school is a religious choice, not an educational choice, on the part of the people choosing to attend these schools. If we are concerned about public schools indoctrinating their students, then certainly these schools make it their main purpose to do so.

The author and his siblings learned that there was "one holy, Catholic and apostolic church" in their 12 years of Catholic schools—a Catholic education that was paid for by our parents and the church we attended. Our non-Catholic friends would disagree with that assertion of the church in my indoctrination into Catholicism. At the time, we did not expect or demand that those fellow citizens contribute to our church school through their state and local taxes. We also had an education devoid of science until 1964. Catholic schools obtain the largest proportion of public dollars as they are organized better than most other religions to do so. In Arizona there are multiple religions running private and charter schools, including the Islamic, Lutheran, Baptist, Christian, Hindu, and Jewish religions. Other religions have dominated the charter market through their ownership by bishops, nuns, ministers, and affiliations with various religious groups' educational programs.

The freedom to "choose" these schools didn't need reinvention. That freedom was debated early along with the idea of financing that freedom of "choice" in our young country.

Freedom to choose was always an option. Who was paying for that individual choice was not.

Private School's Right to Exist and to Educate Children Has Always Been Defended

Early on when the 1919 requirement to educate children was passed, this right of private schools to provide education that met the mandate to educate children in the republic was upheld. In 1925 the case of *Pierce v. Society of Sisters*[2] was settled by the Supreme Court. In brief, Oregon had sought to close all nonpublic schools by not accepting them as meeting the requirement to educate children up to the age of 16. The fact is that this denial of a parent's choice of schools to meet mandatory requirements to educate their children did not stand. Your right to choose has always existed. Your right to state funding for that choice has not, nor was it ever meant to.

Supreme Court cases and legislative efforts that affirmed this separation of church and state are a major topic in *The Troubled Crusade* by Diane Ravitch (1983). The book also chronicles efforts to involve the federal government in local educational funding, which included the Taft Bill and the *Everson v. Board of Education* case taken before the Supreme Court. *Everson*, which allowed municipalities to help with the transportation of children to Catholic schools, was decried by the public.

"Now will Protestants awake?" was heard and written in the press as leaders in the Protestant "Christian" churches made efforts to halt any public funding going to a Catholic school. Imagine their outrage at public vouchers funding Muslim or Jewish private schools, LGBTQ private micro-schools, and other schools now funded through vouchers.

Many of the schools on the list of private schools in Arizona teach in Spanish, a practice that the current superintendent of public instruction has banned in Arizona Public Schools.[3] Not allowed in public schools but OK in private schools.

Shipping a State's Educational Funds to an Out-of-State Provider

A good portion of the funds collected and meant for public common schools within the state wind up in other states' educational marketplaces. All of those out-of-state placements in Arizona went to sectarian organizations in the receiving state (Utah and out-of-state online programs from multiple states). Other countries are also on this gravy train, with internationally based charters and private schools cashing in on the loopholes in our public policy.

The logic used to justify these sectarian choices is that the state is providing voucher reimbursements to the parent. The parents are making the choice of where to spend their windfall from the state. The purchases need to be approved prior to the "vendor" being paid, but the oversight is marginal at best. Micro-schools allow homeschool parents to pay themselves as the guides for their own children and others receiving this version of homeschooling. Of course this applies to sectarian micro-schools also.

The justification and legal backing for this has been based on a June 21, 2022, Supreme Court ruling that a Maine town must pay for a parent's choice to send their child to a Christian high school because the town had always used a local private school as their high school and had funded that "choice." The Court ruled in favor of the parents, 6–3. This ruling ignored precedence for Maine's use of public nonsectarian schools as a choice for parents in districts that did not create public high schools, as well as the stipulations of the separation clause. It also opened the floodgates for equally specious claims for funding in states that had always kept church and state separate. The floodgates were opened, the intent of the party that had appointed the new majority in the Supreme Court while putting a school choice advocate in charge of the Department of Education. Up until this time, the Supreme Court always ruled in favor of the state's right to deny funds for sectarian educations. A similar case in Oregon was decided 5–4, setting the precedent for the Maine case. The 6–3 decision in Maine reflects one justice moving to the yes side because of the *Carson v. Makin* decision. The Oregon precedent was gleefully hailed by the Heritage Foundation, an organization funded by the Coors Foundation and billionaire Richard Mellon Scaife.[4]

Freedom to Choose Was Always a Citizen's Right

In colonial times and after the establishment of our states, communities without publicly funded common schools had several choices. Private schools, religious schools, tutors, plantation schools, and Dame Schools were some of the options available for those with the economic means to pay for those private educations. Dame Schools were similar in scope to the current micro-schools being offered and paid for through the public funding of vouchers.

A citizen's right to choose a private education was not impeded by our public common schools. However, who paid for that individual freedom to choose was clear. Private choices were just that, private.

Homeschooling, with little to no monitoring by the state, was also funded by parents "choosing" to do so rather than the state. Our states all allow parents the option of "homeschooling." Parents are then free to pay themselves as guides to that education when they use micro-schools as the basis for instruction or some online program (mostly sectarian).

What Is Unclear About That Term "Homechooling"?

You chose to school at home, your choice. It is not the public's obligation to fund that personal decision.

The intent of this book is to disprove the fallacy that the freedom to choose where your child attends school was ever impeded. Massachusetts, one of the first states to have public schools, did not require students to attend their common schools if their parents, or community, chose to pay for and send their high school students to attend private schools. There was a brief period where the state would not count Catholic schools as meeting the requirement to educate children in the state. This unjust barrier to a parent's right to choose was quickly and rightly overturned.

What these schools and parents could not count on was funding from the state through scholarships funded by tax exemptions, or what has become known as "universal vouchers" today. Adding insult to injury, most private sectarian schools are nonprofits that do not pay property taxes. Expect micro-schools that are nonprofits to declare the properties where they meet to be eligible for this benefit that nonprofit sectarian and nonsectarian schools are covered under.

A common public education was never meant to be an entitlement to public funding for your personal choice. This entitlement mentality is termed "Friedman's Folly" in this book. Entitlements are, as they should be, antithetical to conservative and libertarian principles. A newcomer to the libertarian cry for less government and more free enterprise is the Koch-funded Americans for Prosperity. Their game plan was outlined by the Libertarian platform when Mr. Koch was their 1980 vice-presidential candidate.

When ALEC (the American Legislative Exchange Council) seeks to lobby our political leaders to privatize education, they argue that our common schools are "government" schools.

This lobbying against government schools is done at the same time that it is lobbying the federal government through the "conservative caucus" to provide funding for "choice." ALEC and the conservative caucus are advocating for diametrically opposed ideas, tax-funded aid for private schools funded by government revenues so parents can be free from government schools.

Mega-charters of over 10,000 students fly in the face of Friedman's complaint that large districts are bureaucratic. If they are, then what are large charter and private school consortiums? You cannot get much more autocratic and bureaucratic than most of our organized religions.

The result is taxation without elected representation in those schools' governing boards. Representation of the taxpayers was always a function of the locally elected school board. What superintendent has never heard the cry, "I'm a taxpayer!" when complaints about the public schools are aired at a public school board meeting? Try the same tactic at a corporate board meeting; they will remind you that they are a private corporation.

The property and funding shift to the private sector is also not what the founders intended when they left education to the states and the people. Educational funding is not an entitlement to public funds for private companies, an idea encapsulated in the idea that children in our republic represent "backpacks full of cash," an oft-used phrase to justify moving the money with the child, as if each child is entitled to our tax funds meant to support public common schools. Billionaires like the idea of privatization because it is an opportunity for them to increase their share of the public's property. They are the investors in those government tax-free bonds tied up in charter IDA bond markets.

A Republic, If You Can Keep It

What many of the founders did suggest and write about was that a common education was needed in order for a republic to survive and prosper. As Benjamin Franklin answered those asking what kind of government we would have: "A republic, if you can keep it." Jefferson pushed for public colleges and to a lesser extent public schools.

> I believe that education is the key to unlocking the full potential of the human mind, and that it should be accessible to all people, regardless of their social class or background.
>
> —Thomas Jefferson

Education is not mentioned in the U.S. Constitution; therefore its establishment as a state or local government-sponsored program is implied by the Tenth Amendment. This critical amendment vests powers in the states and the people for items not covered in the Constitution.

The Tenth Amendment specifically states this:

> The powers not delegated to the United States by the Constitution, nor prohibited by it to the States, are reserved to the States respectively, or to the people.

The "or the people" part of this amendment is often left out by those pushing for states to enact government-paid-for "choice" options in their state. They do this while passing laws diminishing the people's rights to petition the government, a right that is guaranteed in the First Amendment.

We don't interpret the Second Amendment's right to bear arms as a right to obtain funding from the government to purchase those arms. This expenditure of public funds for arms is a justified expenditure of our armed forces when they provide arms to our military forces as part of their equipment.

The Primacy and Economics of Local Control

Interpretations of the Constitution's Tenth Amendment are the main reason most of the funding for education comes from state and local sources. The federal government and its interference in this arrangement through charter grants is the antithesis of local control. In most states, the majority of the funding for common schools still comes from the local (and sometimes county) property taxes that flow to locally controlled, elected boards at locally owned school districts. Local control means locally governed schools. The government control that people have been led to believe exists in our public schools is the local government, the one closest to the people. In New England, many towns still hold school district meetings to discuss and approve the budget and programs of their common schools.

The Bond Market Gets Paid First

Much of the funding that the state government is redirecting to "choice" is being paid directly to financial corporations and private companies. Junk bonds and tax-free bonds arranged by IDA loans use a financial device known as "intercepts," which are direct intercepts of state funding to ensure that the bondholders are paid first, not the privately held school and its students.

Fiscal and Academic Accountability

Private firms and corporate for-profit management firms (domestic and foreign) use related party transactions (accounted for as purchased services in their financials) to move funds from the schools to these for-profit entities. Private school tuitions are not tracked, and private schools (sectarian or not) are not subject to accountability for how they spend their funds or the educational results of their "schools." Many private schools do use standardized testing. The results are not made public. Sectarian private schools are controlled and operated by various religious sects that often have competing visions regarding their religion's primacy and how they should be able to spend the profits from their school enterprises.

Fiscal Oversight Prevents Public Schools From Becoming Overextended

Public common schools' purchases of property and taking on of debt in the public's name are restricted to what the community can afford and what portion of that debt for those properties and the upkeep of those properties the state will pay for. An accepted way of looking at debt-to-assets is by dividing the long-term debt by the value of the business's assets. Figure 2.2 shows the deteriorating debt-to-asset ratio at Arizona charter schools. This is caused by the constant refinancing used to expand, pay off prior owners, and refinance at a better rate. The cut point of .5 defines a good debt-to-asset ratio; anything over .6 is considered high risk, especially when the indebted party loses students, the source of their revenue and the basis of the financial predictions used to pay for their properties. In contrast, our public common schools, which are owned by the public, have tight control on their debt-to-asset ratio. Figure 2.2 illustrates the issue with hard facts on the debt-to-asset ratios for both types of school, public and charter. These figures do not include long-term lease payments or short-term debts assumed by charters during this period.

The concept of school "choice" is an assault on the local control of our common schools by the states and the federal government. "Starving the beast of public education" was an early rallying cry of the legislatures that first proposed "public charter schools." The beast of charter financing of their properties is the greater threat to educational financial stability.

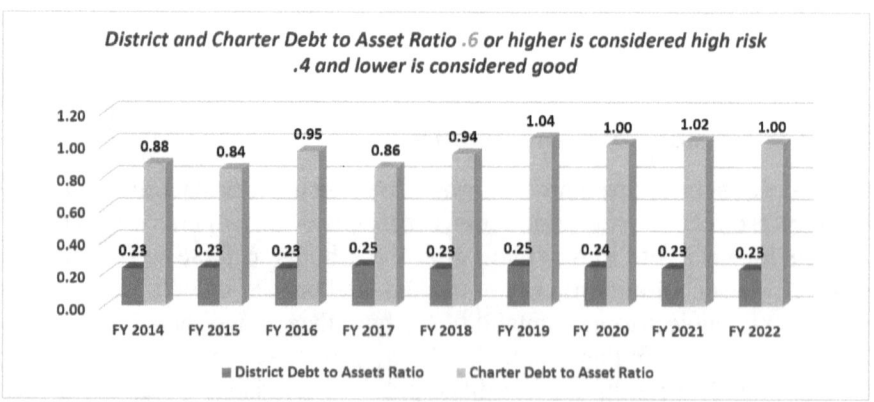

Figure 2.2. Debt-to-Asset Ratio at Arizona Districts and Charters
Source: Superintendents' annual reports from FY 2014–FY 2022, collated by Grand Canyon Institute.

The idea behind starving the beast of public education is that if the legislatures allowed charter schools to be publicly funded choices, then they, the legislatures, would spend less on education. The same logic was used when vouchers and "scholarships" were offered. There are now over 60,000 students in private education programs in Arizona whose parents were paying that tuition cost themselves prior to universal vouchers. How does paying a part of that cost ($8,000 plus) save the state money? Most of the "savings" come from false predictions regarding new private placements by parents in public schools. Left out of those "savings" figures is the fact that the state does not pay full state funding to all of its public schools. That funding is based on a formula keyed to the district's ability to raise property taxes.

Federal Intrusion Into Education

Federal intrusion into the choice debate, while limited, is substantial. This federal factor was clear when PPP and ESSER money became available during the pandemic and "choice" schools, public schools, and churches took those federal funds to meet payroll and day-to-day expenses.

In reality, the federal contribution to all forms of education is currently approximately 8%,[5] (ESSER funding and PPP funds increased this to 16% during COVID for charters and public schools). This federal largesse includes Title I and other title programs and the Department of Agriculture's school lunch program.

This minor fraction of the funding of public education hardly constitutes what is referred to as "government schools" in the writings of Milton Friedman.

Federal Involvement in Education

The National Defense Education Act of 1958, which was a direct response to the Soviet Union's launch of the Sputnik spacecraft, triggered the first direct federal-level spending on education. There wasn't a cabinet-level Department of Education until 1979 when Congress passed legislation sought by Lyndon Johnson, taking education out of the Department of Health, Education, and Welfare. The origin of the Department of Education dates to the administration of Andrew Johnson when the nation was considering making public common schools and educating our newly reformed union (i.e., fulfilling the promise of the Civil War posters extolling blacks to enlist).

Concerns about the amount of science and mathematics our students were being instructed in and about how illiterate most of the Union troops (and Confederate troops) were (a 10% illiteracy rate in our armed forces; this, as we will show, was significantly down from the illiteracy rates of prior generations), along with the promises made to free the slaves and provide public schools for all citizens, led to this establishment of a "Department of Education" at that time. It was not a cabinet-level department.

Federal Money to Any Type of Education Should Be Anathema to "Conservatives"

Barry Goldwater, a staunch conservative, also understood the importance of local control of a tax-funded common education. His ideas regarding our schools are illustrated in his 1960 book *The Conscience of a Conservative* (Goldwater, 1990).

Barry Goldwater openly appreciated the fact that private schools were just that, private. These private choices were similar to the military prep school he attended. Like most of the Greatest Generation, the choice of which school to attend was just that, a personal choice. Payment for that choice rested with the parent electing to choose. Goldwater was also justifiably proud of his military service and rose to the rank of major general in the Air Force Reserve, a fact that most of his critics ignore. While he employed Milton Friedman as an advisor, he and his other advisors often disagreed with Friedman's advice.

We do well to remember that Dr. Friedman's capitalist theories for a republic included his desire to eliminate the Interstate Commerce Commission. He was also an advocate for severe restraints on labor unions. His economic theories have since come under criticism from economists across the political spectrum. So-called "patriots" advocating for choice should know that Friedman also vigorously fought the government's ability to draft people into service during the Vietnam War, equating draftees to "slaves."

CONSERVATIVE OR LIBERAL, FREEDOM COMES WITH RESPONSIBILITY

"With great freedom comes great responsibility."—Eleanor Roosevelt
Friedman's Folly: Education in a Republic is an Entitlement to Government Funding

- We will argue that public education is not, nor was it ever intended to be, an entitlement to public funding for a private education or your choice to "homeschool."
- We will show that we have always had the option to pay for our freedom to choose sectarian or private educations for our children. When that right was challenged, the courts ruled in favor of a parent's right to choose, not for public payment for that choice.

Modern so-called conservatives and libertarians bent on creating what they call "free market choices" financed by the public have created an entitlement mind-set. In their efforts to privatize education, they have confused our economic system, capitalism, with our political system, a democratic republic. There is an important difference between our economic system and the governance of our republic. Our republic guarantees liberty and justice for all, not freedom to choose.

Freedom to choose my options in life is a personal issue with personal costs. I can choose to pave my driveway, but I can't deduct the cost of that driveway or expect my town to pay for it because they fund other roadways. I am required to have smoke detectors in my newly constructed home. The local fire department is not required to pay for that cost even though the town mandated the requirement. I am not free to choose not to have this required feature in my home at my expense.

"Choice" advocacy groups cite the work of Milton Friedman to defend their quest to capture public funding for private educational providers with little to no oversight regarding the quality of that education or how that money is spent. Freedom of choice has been sold as a right of individual parents to common funding sources to pay for that freedom.

The ultimate goal of these free market education ideas is that all parents pay for their own child's education. A full reading of Friedman's writings makes this final phase of personal choice clear.

In regard to federal involvement in this scheme, advocates of "choice" have forgotten the wisdom of Barry Goldwater who knew that "he who pays the piper calls the tune." When Senator Goldwater spoke against the National Defense of Education Act, he noted, "This legislation will mark the inception of aid, supervision, and ultimately control of education in this country by federal authorities."[6]

It must be with tongue in cheek that the Center for Educational Reform, a charter and choice advocacy group, published an article titled "Restoring Federalism in Education: The Charter State Option"[7] in reaction to the Bush-era testing mandates in No Child Left Behind. Seeking to restore federalism is presented as proper government involvement in our educational programs.

Since the early 1990s the country has been moving toward a financial model in education that is a throwback to what is referred to as the "good old days" prior to a common publicly funded education becoming available to all students in 1919. This nostalgic and skewed look at American education prior to public schools is the theme of *Market Education* (Coulson, 1999), a book that glorifies market solutions to educational issues currently besetting the republic by citing examples from our republic prior to common schools for all.

"Private choices" have evolved to become vouchers and direct contracts with parents to private and religious organizations. These funds, no matter who the go-between is, are being paid for by tax revenues, revenues that were raised to provide for a common education. Any other expenditure is a misappropriation of funding.

In this book, we refer to this entitlement notion as "Friedman's Folly." Friedman justified this expenditure of public funds on privately held schools using what he termed the "neighborhood effect,"[8] a theory that was popular at the time he proposed his model for school choice. The neighborhood effect is the antithesis of what we refer to as "Horace's Hope." Horace Mann hoped to raise up the entire community, one neighborhood at a time, with that neighborhood controlling the local schools held in common through its elected boards.

Promoters of Friedman's model of competition to improve the academic performance at our schools often cite that even though states continue to increase their spending on education in each locality based on *Serrano v. Priest*,[9] which challenged districts' reliance on property taxes as unfair to localities with a low tax base, those schools have not substantially improved their academic performance.

Efforts to work through the courts to ensure that states contributed adequately to public common schools through equalization formulas were rampant in the 1980s. At the same time, Federal Law 94–142 (1976) created an obligation to educate children with learning disabilities and physical handicaps from age 3 to 21. When critics of our public schools cite the lack of academic performance gains with additional funding from equalization and adequacy formulas in the states, they fail to consider the implications of educating all of our children as mandated by 94–142.

This performance issue was used to promote "No Child Left Behind" (NCLB) legislation demanding higher academic performance or else risk losing federal dollars for education. Under NCLB, parents could take their share of federal dollars and spend them with private contractors. Considering the expanded role in educating every child and the additional costs for this that districts absorbed, these new requirements consumed greater and greater shares of our common schools budgets. Friedman often noted that the increase in spending went to administration, ignoring the fact that entire new special education departments had to be created to meet the demands of 94.142. Private schools have no such obligation under these laws and can reject students if they don't meet the school's admission or retention (i.e., academic standards that must be met to stay at the school) criteria.

Horace's Hope

A new republic called for an educated public and a new model for education designed specifically for citizens in a republic. Horace Mann knew that public education was and should be a function of a local school board and the individual state's department of education. He knew that it might look different from state to state. Local control ensures that difference and that community norms are important elements of education.

Horace Mann, the father of American public education and common schools, developed and articulated the system of public education we have via common locally governed schools. Many critics of Mann's work confuse his study of the Prussian and British systems of education with wholesale adoption of those models. Mann's model for common schools was specifically and intentionally set up for educating all citizens so that all citizens had the means to fully participate as citizens of the republic.

How easily we forget that most of the world was uneducated and living under the rule of monarchs when Mann proposed his common school model. We forget that the king or queen of England was and is also the head of the Church of England.

It was advantageous for those in power as monarch to ensure that the public under that type of governmental structure was uneducated regarding their own rights. Teaching the monarch's subjects about the divine rights of kings was part of the education there. Even current artificial intelligence searches on this topic understand this: "The idea of separating the church and the state was influenced by the opposition to the English episcopal system and the English throne, as well as by the Enlightenment ideals of reason and natural rights. It was also implemented in France as a result of the social-revolutionary criticism of the wealthy ecclesiastical hierarchy and the desire to guarantee the freedom of the church."[10]

Laws in our early history made it illegal to educate slaves. A real innovator in education in the 1800s and to this day, Horace Mann has been assailed by those hoping to return to private, segregated, religiously controlled educational models.[11] They expect and demand that this personal "choice" be paid for by public funds.

The status quo at the time that Horace Mann was setting up common schools was segregated, private education paid for by the children's parents. This time around, the privatizers want their private education paid for by the public via tax-credit scholarships, vouchers, and state contracts with charter schools, with the privately owned facilities paid for by tax-free bonds that benefit the bottom line of Wall Street and in many cases overseas investors.

Hedge fund managers and other millionaires have spent millions of dollars endorsing candidates who support school choice. Tax-free earnings on junk bonds funding their investment in charter and private school properties are the reward for their political largesse. Overleveraged and cash-strapped charter schools are the result.

Public education (i.e., common schools) were designed to be locally controlled and state and locally funded. To this day, most federal funding still comes with the caveat that federal funds must "supplement, not supplant," those elements of education that should be paid for by the state and local communities. As noted, the first real infusion of federal funds for education occurred when the National Defense Education Act of 1958 provided funding and loans to higher-education programs after the Russians' successful launch of Sputnik. In contrast to this limited federal role in education, the federal and state governments have been actively financing and enabling, through tax-free bonds and now (as of 2021) guaranteed bond financing, privately owned educational organizations and facilities with public dollars.

Enough Already!

The federal funds for programs such as Title I and other supplemental programs at our elementary and high schools were not meant to constitute an entitlement program. They are specifically set up to supplement local funding for a common education for the general public.

Local control and the "will of the people" have been undercut by changes in the way 27 states are now funding their new definitions of what constitutes a "publicly funded education" and their interpretation of precedents by the current Supreme Court. One of the unexpected results of states' equalization of funding and adequacy decisions was that they created a way for states to use those funds to subcontract education to privately owned charter schools and private sectarian and nonsectarian schools via vouchers tied to a percentage of state funding. The same funding goes to students in wealthy communities as to communities with middle-income and poorer families.

The proponents of these changes view state and federal educational funding as an entitlement program for individual "choice" under these new definitions of public school choice. Promoters of the privatization movement call this "freedom of choice" and talk about educational funding as if it is an entitlement. These groups and their advocates in the state legislatures and Congress cavalierly speak of education funding as "backpacks full of cash" that should follow students to their parents' school of choice. They have created the belief among parents interested in collecting money for their child's private education that they are entitled to this funding. This belief flows from the efforts of privatizers insisting that parents have a right to a paid-for "choice."

After over a quarter of a century of "choice," the overwhelming choice of the public (85%) has continued to be the local school district in states with charter schools, "opportunity scholarships," and voucher programs.

The public as a whole has seen that charter schools and vouchers are a scheme to eliminate the public from public education. What they still remain blind to is that the goal of privatizers and capitalist theorists regarding education is to eventually make educational expenses a private matter, with the parents responsible for paying for their child's education.

Make no mistake. This is what market education is ultimately about: parents in the future will pay for their own child's education.

This is referred to by the innocuous name of "market education." It is an economic model for educating our children, not an educational model. A thorough reading of Friedman's work exposes this ultimate goal of privatization of education.

Ultimately There Is No Free Lunch: The End Game of Friedman's Free Market Choice

Friedman's early writings always implied that once market education had taken over, parents would take care to only have children if they could afford to pay for their child's education. This would limit their reproductive choices to those children that they could afford. This, then, is the ultimate goal of the privatization movement: parents pay for their children's education. This is "enlightened" reproduction by privately educated parents.

As stated in Friedman's (1962/1990) original paper titled "Free to Choose": "Ultimately, parents make the choice of whether to educate their children and in the end will pay for their children's education."

Market education has been tried before. The reality was that parents of poor children mostly opted to have their children go to work to help support the family, an economic choice. It is no coincidence that the current round of easing child labor laws in Republican states is anticipating a regression to the myth of the success of market education from the past. The logic is that those children will be homeschooled or use online private and charter schools to "enable" them to work and go to "school" at the same time. The rise of "micro-schools" is the first phase of this elimination of the working class from our public schools.

Illiteracy, which has been all but erased in our republic since public common schools became available to all, will return if we abandon Horace's hope for education in our democratic republic for an economic model based on a capitalist vision for education.

What Did a Real Conservative Believe About Free Markets and Education?

Barry Goldwater believed in the benefits of a free market economy. He also expressed concerns about how the public education system in the United States was performing, suggesting a way to refocus, not replace, our common schools' efforts. He was correct in his analysis.

> We have encouraged the teaching profession to be more concerned with how a subject is taught than with what is taught. Most important of all: in our anxiety to "improve" the world and insure "progress" we have permitted our schools to become laboratories for social and economic change according to the predilections of the professional educators.
>
> It is the fashion these days to say that responsibility for education "traditionally" rests with the local community—as a prelude to proposing an exception to the tradition in the form of federal aid.
>
> We have forgotten that the proper function of the school is to transmit the cultural heritage of one generation to the next generation, and to so train the minds of the new generation as to make them capable of absorbing ancient learning and applying it to the problem of its own day.
>
> We have forgotten that purpose of education. Or better: we have forgotten for whom education is intended. The function of our schools is not to educate, or elevate society; but rather to educate individuals and equip them with the knowledge that will enable them to take care of society's needs.
>
> We have forgotten that a society progresses only to the extent that it produces leaders that are capable of guiding and inspiring progress. And we cannot develop such leaders unless our standards of education are geared to excellence instead of mediocrity.

Researching every paper and book by Barry Goldwater, one cannot find any quote attributed to him endorsing the idea of vouchers or charter schools. In conversations (June 5, 2023) with Mr. Goldwater's closest relative, the author confirmed this research result. The idea of weakening local control of education was not in his platform in 1964, which including the following points:

- To continue the advancement of education on all levels, through such programs as selective aid to higher education and strengthened state and local tax resources, including tax credits for college education, while resisting Democratic efforts that endanger local control of schools.
- To help assure equal opportunity and a good education for all, while opposing federally sponsored "inverse discrimination," whether by the shifting of jobs, or the abandonment of neighborhood schools, for reasons of race. (Taken from the Republican Platform of 1964)[12]

Why then is the Goldwater Institute's stance on "choice" so fixated on this economic vision of privately controlled public schools? It is clear that this entity is not representing the stated views of its namesake who clearly felt that education was the purview of locally controlled public schools and people's ability to go, at their own expense, to private schools.

Senator Goldwater abhorred federal involvement in education, which he made abundantly clear during his political life. This despite his friendship with Milton Friedman who served as an advisor to the Goldwater campaign in the 1960s. The references to economic freedom and individual freedom in the Republican platform were most likely influenced by Friedman.

Another Economist Enters the Fray About Privatizing Public Education

The Goldwater Institute's approval of and support for charter schools and choice occurred during the tenure of Michael Block, an accomplished entrepreneur and a noted economist, as the institute's president. Dr. Block was president of the Goldwater Institute from 1992 to 2002. Dr. Block (who holds a PhD in economics from Stanford) also served as senior policy advisor to Arizona governor Fife Symington in 1996 and 1997. The institute's involvement in "choice" and the numerous papers it produces on this topic continue to this day. The issue has become a major part of their reports to the public and their efforts in the press.

In order to prove his theories on educational funding and to illustrate the type of schools he was advocating, Dr. Block and his wife, Olga Block, went on to found BASIS charter and private schools in 1998. BASIS is a high-performing school that serves students in Arizona, Washington, and other states. It also has international sites in China. BASIS is currently (2023) managed by BASIS Educational Ventures, a for-profit firm. Their educational performance is beyond reproach, and they manage their schools in a fiscally sound manner. The firm's management group is a for-profit entity, and their audits are unavailable to the public.

The Politics of "Choice"

Politically, the biggest influencer supporting "the freedom to choose" nationally is the American Legislative Exchange (ALEC). ALEC was formed in 1973 as a direct result of Senator Goldwater's defeat in 1964 by the Democratic candidate, Lyndon Johnson. ALEC and the conservative caucuses nationally and at the state level champion "school choice" and work with national and state political leaders involved with the efforts to create "the freedom to choose."

The ALEC namesake was introduced in 1975. ALEC functions as a conservative think tank and introduces what it deems to be model legislation for state legislators and private sector members to collaborate on as model bills to introduce in their states. A major goal of the organization is to privatize functions traditionally left to the local, state, and federal government in our republic. They are "free market" enthusiasts confusing our form of government with our economic system in our republic. There are also many pro-choice organizations drawing their financial support from the bond markets, as well as other "conservative" groups pushing the public toward believing that a right to choose and to collect funding for that choice exists. Christian nationalists are also proponents of a parent's right to choose a sectarian private school and to collect vouchers to pay for part of the tuition and other costs. Most state constitutions still have language banning such transfers of state funds to religious organizations. Currently, several states have Christian schools trying to set up charter schools. The Catholic Church has proposed an online charter in several states that would serve children in multiple states.

The logic used for bypassing a state constitution's ban on aid to sectarian schools by paying the parent for accepted voucher expenses via a "ClassWallet"[13] type of program set up for this type of transaction does not hold up. A previous Supreme Court ruled in favor of the state of Washington when it exempted payment to a divinity school student from the state's post–high school scholarship funding. *Locke v. Davey* in 2004 prohibited the use of a state scholarship to pay for a divinity degree for the student who received the scholarship. The Court ruled that the state was correct in disallowing this use of state funds to fund a sectarian education that graduated ministers with divinity degrees.

Pseudo-Conservative Majority on the U.S. Supreme Court

Things changed after a "conservative majority" took over the Supreme Court.

The Institute for Justice, an organization dedicated to judicial activism and school choice,[14] represented the plaintiffs in the Maine case of *Carson v. Makin*, receiving a 6–3 ruling in favor of the plaintiff's right to funding for their choice of a religious school. Maine had a generous provision for parents choosing which school to attend ($11,500) when a town elected to send their students to a private school that contracted with that town for high school. The school selected for funding was nonsectarian. These arrangements have a historical context. They were voted on by the townspeople when they decided to forgo building their own public high school.

In the Maine case, the Court relied on its decisions in *Trinity Lutheran Church of Columbia v. Comer* (2017) and *Espinoza v. Montana Department of Revenue* (2020). In *Trinity Lutheran*, the Court held that Missouri could not discriminate against otherwise eligible recipients of public benefits because of their religion. The benefits sought were for a sectarian preschool with a kindergarten program. This is one of the largest portions of spending in states with scholarship funds and vouchers. Parents are using the vouchers for preschool programs that they formerly paid for out of pocket. Preschool and in some states kindergarten are not part of a free and appropriate education unless the child in question has been identified through Child Find. Child Find is part of the 1976 IDEA Law (Public Law 94–142, the Individuals with Disabilities Education Act).[15] In FY 2022, 20.3% of all funding for "scholarships" went to preschool and kindergarten private schools. Many of these were day-care providers that previously had been private companies offering paid-for day care at a premium price.

In *Espinoza*, the Court held unconstitutional (5–4) a provision of the Montana Constitution that barred aid to a school "controlled in whole or in part by any church, sect, or denomination." These cases have been used to overturn provisions to separate church and state that are in the Constitution and to force states to modify their own constitution's rules regarding the same.

Talk about federal intrusion into local matters. Cases unrelated to school but empowering a business's right to discriminate based on their religious choices (e.g., providing services to LGBTQ consumers) have emboldened the religious right. State rules for voucher-paid institutions do not list all of the categories for which the schools must allow equal access in their "businesses."

Horace Mann would agree with Senator Goldwater's statements regarding the purpose of education and for whom that education is intended. He would be vehemently opposed to the capitalistic model that advocates of the "freedom to choose" lobby endorse. These lobbying groups believe that capitalism is our economic model while forgetting that a democratic republic is our method of governing ourselves. Capitalism does not trump democracy. His stance on public funding for sectarian education (and the stance of the founders) is described in later chapters.

Horace's hope and his intent was to develop locally controlled common schools that would provide that type of moral common education as an opportunity to all of the children in the republic. It is time to get back to that model and the founders' vision for public common schools. It is time we took financial responsibility for our religious choices.

NOTES

1. https://www.educationnext.org/news-parents-voice-concern-sale-basis-independent-schools
2. https://www.oyez.org/cases/1900-1940/268us510
3. The attempt by the superintendent of public instruction to keep state funds from these schools has been challenged and is in the courts.
4. https://www.heritage.org/education/report/carson-v-makin-the-supreme-court-closed-the-book-religious-discrimination-school
5. This figure went to 16% as the federal government provided extra funding via the PPP program and direct loans to public and charter schools. https://www.federalpay.org/paycheck-protection-program. This was followed by the ESSER I, II, and III loan programs (see https://oese.ed.gov/offices/education-stabilization-fund/elementary-secondary-school-emergency-relief-fund) that de facto saved the charter marketplace. Charter promoters complain that ESSER funding benefited public schools more than charters.
6. https://www.cato.org/commentary/those-who-wanted-federal-power-over-schools-now-fear-betsy-devos-might-use-it-foster
7. https://edreform.com/2006/11/restoring-federalism-in-education-the-charter-state-option-dan-lips
8. http://precaution.org/lib/friedman_role_of_government_in_schools.1955.pdf
9. https://repository.uclawsf.edu/cgi/viewcontent.cgi?article=2213&context=hastings_law_journal
10. http://law.cornell.edu.
11. Center on Education Policy, 2020, *History and Evolution of Public Education in the United States*, https://files.eric.ed.gov/fulltext/ED606970.pdf
12. *Republican Party Platform of 1964*, American Presidency Project, https://www.presidency.ucsb.edu/documents/republican-party-platform-1964
13. https://classwallet.com
14. https://www.econtalk.org/clint-bolick-defends-judicial-activism
15. https://www.govinfo.gov/content/pkg/STATUTE-89/pdf/STATUTE-89-Pg773.pdf

REFERENCES

Coulson, A. J. (1999). *Market education: The unknown history*. New Brunswick, NJ: Transaction Publishers.

Friedman, M., and R. D. Friedman (1990). *Free to choose: A personal statement*. San Diego: Harcourt Brace Jovanovich. (Original work published 1962)

Goldwater, B. M. (1990). *The conscience of a conservative*. Washington, DC: Regnery. (Original work published 1960)

Chapter 3

"The Public Should No Longer Remain Ignorant"

The privatization of public education via "school choice" has been a political issue since the finding that separate is not equal, which overturned *Plessey v. Ferguson*, was made by the Supreme Court in *Brown v. Board of Education* in 1954. It is important to note that privatization is a political rather than an educational issue.

In the current political environment, a reversal of *Brown* by the Supreme Court, like the reversal of *Roe v. Wade*, and rulings in favor of a parent's right to send their child to a religious school at taxpayer expense would not be a surprise. If the powers pushing for school choice have their way, freedom to choose will trump equalization of opportunity.

Milton Friedman called this "freedom to choose."

WE HAVE ALWAYS BEEN FREE TO CHOOSE

Our ability to be "free to choose" where we attend school was always a fact since the earliest stirrings of our republic.

What was never a fundamental freedom was the freedom to take public funds to support our personal choice.

Publicly paid for education is not an entitlement. For groups that consider themselves "conservatives" to treat it as such in their demand for the "right to choose" is anathema to true conservative thinking, which has always considered local control a vital aspect of public education.

Catholic parents, like those of the author, were always free to send their children to a Catholic school. (As noted, this was not the case when public schools were first started in Massachusetts.) They expected that they would pay for that freedom to choose and also contribute to those who could not afford the tuition in their parish. They also knew that it was their duty, as citizens, to fund the public schools in our town.

The price of that Catholic school tuition was artificially low at the time because most of the teachers in the 1950s and early 1960s were nuns or brothers. Our church called this choice, and the choice to teach as a layperson at a Catholic school was a "sacrifice" for our faith. Retirement plans for those teachers come nowhere near meeting the teachers' retirement needs. In New Hampshire and several other states, the church does not provide any retirement benefits for teachers in their schools. This is the case for my son who teaches mathematics at the local Catholic high school after leaving his profession as a nuclear engineer. As he notes, his bonuses used to be more than his current yearly salary.

The Catholic Church has the largest network of private schools in the United States. Total Catholic school enrollment was 1.9 million in FY 2017. Catholic schools pre-date the Revolution, especially in the far south, which was controlled by Spain and France at the time, both Catholic nations. When New Hampshire implemented vouchers for public schools, my grandchildren, whose parents had always paid for their education along with donations from their own parents, received a state voucher in FY 2022 for part of the cost of that education. Again, these children were never being paid for by the general public before.

During the time when Horace Mann was elected as the first secretary of the newly created Massachusetts Board of Education, the public schools in Massachusetts were experiencing an influx of students who had never been exposed to an education of any type. A large portion of those children were Irish Catholics. Children were also working in mills and on farms, supplementing their family's finances, as child labor laws did not exist at that time. Naturally, an influx of new students with limited education delivered early educators a clientele that was mentally able to learn but was deprived of an environment that was rich in educational opportunities.

British public schools experienced this same influx of unprepared students from mills in England, which caused a temporary decline in literacy in Britain. The result being that the British made public education mandatory.

THE BRITISH EXPERIENCE

After a steep decline in literacy in England during the nineteenth century the British made education compulsory towards the end of the 1800s. Rising educational provision—especially for working class children—was one of the primary factors that accounted for the steep and steady decline in illiteracy in Britain during the nineteenth century. However, it must be borne in mind that people also picked up and honed the ability to read and write through other means, including learning and practicing at home and through extended education. Moreover, education was not made compulsory and free until the end of the nineteenth century, so the initiative for schooling largely lay with the parents. Thus, the simple provision of education does not explain the whole story behind rising literacy rates during the nineteenth century; the initiative of parents and children is important as well.

The sum total of these efforts was a steady drop in illiteracy rates throughout the period—even before the introduction of the state system of elementary education in 1870.[1] In 1800 around 40 percent of males and 60 percent of females in England and Wales were illiterate. By 1840 this had decreased to 33 percent of men and 50 percent of women, and, by 1870, these rates had dropped further still to 20 percent of men and 25 percent of women. By the turn of the century, illiteracy rates for both sexes had dropped to around 3 percent. Throughout most of the nineteenth century, Scotland, with its different education system, had lower illiteracy rates; in 1855, for example, only 11 percent of men and 23 percent of women were illiterate. However, by the late nineteenth century, the gap between England, Wales and Scotland had narrowed and closed. . . . The rise in literacy in nineteenth-century Britain led to an increase in the size of the reading public. Most of the rise was confined to the working classes and, as such, impacted them the most, enabling more and more people to write letters (allowing them to maintain relationships outside their immediate localities), fill their leisure hours with the reading of imaginative fiction and newspapers, expand their employment opportunities, and follow and participate in politics. Developments in the newspaper press during this period thus went hand-in-hand with these changes in education and literacy, which created new markets and new audiences.[2]

THE GREATEST GENERATION UNDERSTOOD THE IMPORTANCE OF A COMMON PUBLIC EDUCATION

The first generation of Americans to benefit from a nationwide public education were in common public schools during the period between 1919 and 1924. We refer to this generation as "the Greatest Generation" (Brokaw, 2005). This generation realized that common public schools where citizenship was actively taught united the citizens of this country as equal partners in the republic's future. When they returned from the Second World War and Korea, they continued to serve their communities as school board members, town council members, and at the state and national level as members of legislative and executive branches of government. This generation also voted down state efforts to create a voucher system to finance private educations.

The government referred to in the derisive term "government schools" is the government of our public schools and their locally elected school boards.

School boards are closest to our purest form of democratic representation (Thurber, 1945). In New England, where public common schools started, public school district meetings to approve or disapprove the budget are still held in our public spaces in front of local voters.

One has to completely ignore the public record to conclude that public education has been a "failure" in the United States. Bracey, along with others, has debunked the statistics in *A Nation at Risk* in person, at national seminars, and in his writings (Bracey, 1997, 2002, 2003, 2004).

As a young teacher in the 1970s and a 1974 graduate of one of Horace Mann's original normal schools (Salem State College, now the University of Massachusetts at Salem), I became intrigued with the calls to go back to "the good old days" of education in the United States. I have used the statistics in the chart labeled "Percentage of Persons 14 Years Old and Over Who Were Illiterate" to make a point about how those "good old days" weren't so good.

So, who is pushing this idea of "market education" being so successful in the past?

In his book *Market Education: The Unknown History*, Andrew J. Coulson (1999) derisively writes, "In 1841, Horace Mann, the godfather of American public schooling, promised: 'Let the Common School be expanded to its capabilities,' let it be worked with the efficiency of which it is susceptible, and nine tenths of the crimes in the penal code would become obsolete; the long catalogue of human ills would be abridged."

Coulson then writes, "In 1998, the Los Angeles County School Board voted to arm its public school police with shotguns," citing the public records of the LA School Board. The murder rate at the time of this action was 6.3 per 100,000. In 2021 the rate is 6.5 per 100,000. It was 9.8 in 1998.[3]

He then asks, "Has public schooling failed?" as if the assignment of guards to public schools, which was always a practice at private schools along with gated entries, is an indication of the failure of educating the masses.

In his next reference to Horace Mann, Coulson calls him "a romantic nineteenth century crusader." This quip is really a poke at Mann's "romantic views," which included improving the lot of the mentally ill in Massachusetts in his first public role, and his "romantic view" that slavery should be abolished and women treated as equal citizens to men.

Coulson then goes on to praise the merits and effectiveness of market education as practiced in this country prior to universal public education in 1919. Historic data does not back up his assertions.

The real tell in the historic record is the country's literacy rates. If we look at literacy rates in the United States from 1870 to 1979, the efficacy of our public schools versus market-based education becomes clear. A rising tide raised all boats when public common schools became available to all.

Like the Royal Astronomer in Thurber's "The Royal Astronomer" (a short story in his book *The White Deer*, 1945), the Cato Institute's director of the Center for Educational Reform looks back at history with nostalgic eyes blinded by a desire to convince the reader that while a common public education has failed, there once was a golden age when private market–based education ruled. On page 95 of his well-researched but faultily constructed book, Coulson makes use of David Mitch's work on literacy rates in England to make claims regarding the literacy rates at private versus public schools (Mitch, 1982, 1992). This is followed up by citing Vincent's work on the reduction of literacy in the church-run public schools in England (Vincent, 1989, 2000). The conclusion, of course, is that private schools beat out public schools.

What does the historical record really have to say about literacy in our republic? Table 3.1 focuses on U.S. literacy rates since 1870.

For those who are averse to statistical data and still believe in the "good old days" when high schools were places of learning free from gun violence, we suggest looking at the classic film about those good old days, *Rebel Without a Cause*, or the version regarding British Schools, *To Sir With Love*. Despite the tumultuous road that public education has taken in this republic, literacy rates and high school graduation rates for all categories of students have both risen dramatically with the rise of public education.[4]

Table 3.1. Percentage of persons 14 years old and over who were illiterate (unable to read or write in any language), by race and nativity: 1870 to 1979

Year	Total	White			Black and other
		Total	Native	Foreign-born	
1870	20.0	11.5	–	–	79.9
1880	17.0	9.4	8.7	12.0	70.0
1890	13.3	7.7	6.2	13.1	56.8
1900	10.7	6.2	4.6	12.9	44.5
1910	7.7	5.0	3.0	12.7	30.5
1920	6.0	4.0	2.0	13.1	23.0
1930	4.3	3.0	1.6	10.8	16.4
1940	2.9	2.0	1.1	9.0	11.5
1947	2.7	1.8	–	–	11.0
1950	3.2	–	–	–	–
1952	2.5	1.8	–	–	10.2
1959	2.2	1.6	–	–	7.5
1969	1.0	0.7	–	–	3.6*
1979	0.6	0.4	–	–	1.6*

1870 Based on black population only

Source: U.S. Department of Commerce, Bureau of the Census, Historical Statistics of the United States, Colonial Times to 1970; and Current Population Reports, Series P-23, Ancestry and Language in the United States: November 1979. (This table was prepared in September 1992.)

Are our public common schools perfect? No. They are, however, the quickest proven route to meeting Horace Mann's first goal for a common education in our young republic: that "the public should no longer remain ignorant."

NOTES

1. Original footnote: "Historians have been able to estimate literacy rates in nineteenth century Britain by analyzing marriage registers. Under Lord Hardwick's Marriage Act of 1754, only marriages that were recorded in Church of England registers were legal; this required the signature of the bride, bridegroom and two witnesses. In 1836, a system of secular state registration was introduced. Using these registers, historians have been able to measure literacy rates by calculating how many people were able to sign their names. While a somewhat imperfect measure, it does provide a general indication regarding changes in literacy rates throughout the period."

2. https://www.gale.com/binaries/content/assets/gale-us-en/primary-sources/intl-gps/intl-gps-essays/full-ghn-contextual-essays/ghn_essay_bln_lloyd3_website.pdf

3. https://www.brennancenter.org/our-work/research-reports/myths-and-realities-understanding-recent-trends-violent-crime

4. https://nces.ed.gov/programs/coe/indicator/coi/high-school-graduation-rates

REFERENCES

Brokaw, T. 2005. *Greatest generation.* New York: Random House.

Coulson, A. J. (1999). *Market education: The unknown history.* New Brunswick, NJ: Transaction Publishers.

Chapter 4

Horace's Hope and Intent

For the ideals espoused by the founders regarding the establishment of a public education in our new republic to be realized, it would take men and women who were deeply connected to the founders and the great thinkers during this dawn of American freedom and liberty.

That unique person was a young, successful lawyer from Franklin, Massachusetts, named Horace Mann. His commitment to education in a republic is spelled out in his book *The Republic and the School*. In this work he connects Benjamin Franklin's oft-repeated quote, "A republic, if you can keep it," to the need for common public schools in that republic.

Horace Mann had a deep connection to this period in our history. His brother-in-law, Nathaniel Hawthorne, and he were both married to Peabody sisters. The Peabody sisters cowrote *Moral Culture of Literacy and Kindergarten Guide* in 1863 after Horace's death. The title of the book ties morality to literacy, a theme of Horace Mann's work. Louise Tharp's book *Until Victory*, a biography of Horace Mann, is a well-researched telling of the story of Horace Mann and Mary Peabody (Tharp, 1953) that gives insights into what motivated this key figure in American public education.

Other influences on Horace's philosophical approach to education were William Ellery Channing, Lucretia Mott, Hannah May Longshore, and many of the abolitionists of the early 1800s, including Harriet Beecher Stowe and Henry Ward Beecher. Though there were many key players in our early efforts to create a public common school education model, Horace Mann stands out as an exemplar.

Horace Mann was:

- A person so highly regarded by the Whig Party, and connected to the founders' intent for public education, that he was the person chosen by the party to take John Quincy Adams's seat in Congress when Adams died in February 1848.

- A person who would intentionally design a system for financing and implementing a common public education at the state and local levels in the new American republic without regard to his own personal financial interests.
- A lawyer who was selected to represent the defendants during the Pearl Incident[1] trial in 1848, the largest attempted escape by the Underground Railroad and the cause of two days of intense rioting in Washington, DC.

Horace Mann intentionally laid out what a public common education was to provide in order to encourage the development of freethinking, moral, educated citizens in all economic strata of our republic. He sought, as he often admonished others to do, "to be ashamed to die before winning some small victory for mankind."

That victory was a public common education designed for our republic (Tharp, 1953).

SIX PRINCIPLES FOR A COMMON EDUCATION

Horace Mann laid out six core principles regarding the republic's interest in funding, governing, and controlling a common public education sustained by an interested public at the local level.

1. The public should no longer remain ignorant.
2. That such education should be paid for, controlled, and sustained by an interested public.
3. That this education will be best provided in schools that embrace children from a variety of backgrounds.
4. That this education must be nonsectarian.
5. That this education must be taught by the spirit, methods, and discipline of a free society.
6. That education should be provided by well-trained, professional teachers.

During his tenure as Massachusetts' first secretary of public education, Mann worked for:

- More and better-equipped common schoolhouses built at public expense.
- Longer school years covering more years of schooling (until 16 years old).
- Higher pay for teachers.
- An educated teaching force that would learn their craft at two-year "normal schools" established by the state of Massachusetts and other states.
- A wider curriculum beyond reading, writing, and arithmetic.

- An end to corporal punishment as a means of controlling classroom discipline (the statement "spare the rod, spoil the child" was pushback from the educators and church leaders of his time who wanted to continue the practice of using a rod[2] and humiliating students [think dunce caps] in order to control behavior).

Mann was active in efforts to limit and outlaw slavery. He was intentional about where Massachusetts set up normal schools, advocating the choice of Salem, Massachusetts, because of the city's policy of educating all its citizens, including all races and creeds. Salem, Massachusetts, at the time was the premier port in America, and many of the sailors in its shipyards were freed, prosperous, middle-class blacks and New England tribesmen. The town was not repeating its past errors of relying on religious rule in its schools and system of courts (think Salem witch trials).

The Effort to Traduce and Downplay Horace Mann's Principles of Education

Promoters of what they themselves term "free market" education practices make it a part of their underlying strategy to discredit and traduce Horace Mann's principles of education. They do this by advocating for a capitalistic business model based on private ownership of schools rather than an educational model based on local control by a local governing board—a capitalistic versus a democratic republic's model of common education.

The "free market" model was postulated and promoted by Milton Friedman in the mid-20th century. We already knew what the "free market" model looked like. The country experienced the results of "market education" based on the consumer's ability to pay for that education during its early years prior to tax-funded free common schools. We had also experienced the results of unfettered capitalism and monopolistic price fixing and realized that unfettered capitalism needed some restraints.

The result of a market-based education system was that the majority of people remained uneducated and unaware of their rights and responsibilities in a republic. Their ability to read and write was at a historic low. In addition, the teaching of slaves was prohibited in the South while slaveholders hired private teachers to educate their own children and other plantation owners' children at the plantation. Women hardly fared better, with some Dame Schools set up specifically to educate young ladies.

Accountability and Academic Performance Issues

The other thing that is cited by "choice" advocates is that the only way to change how public schools that are failing work is through marketplace competition. The thing being debated is holding public schools accountable for their students' academic performance and achievement. Dr. Ray Budde, the education professor who proposed the idea of charter schools, had a noncapitalistic method to do just that. His obituary[3] noted:

> Dr. Budde, a former assistant professor at the school of education at the University of Massachusetts, Amherst, first suggested the term "charter" for use in education in the 1970s to describe a novel contracting arrangement designed to support the efforts of innovative teachers within the public school system. He long opposed the later idea that charter schools could be an alternative to public education.

The model was meant to create public charter common schools where innovation thrived.

Charters Using Dr. Budde's Model Were Supported by the Unions

Another charge made by those promoting choice is that the teachers' unions are blocking innovations and the choice model. An early supporter of charters, as described by Dr. Budde, was Albert Shanker and the American Federation of Teachers. The unions withdrew that support after the new model made those charters private enterprises with no local control. During my career, I have witnessed many teachers and administrators who have gone beyond the bounds imposed by a "traditional education." An example that made national news was Dr. Dennis Littky, who transformed education at Thayer High School. At the time, I was the principal at the adjoining elementary school in Winchester, New Hampshire. Dennis was fired and then reinstated when the school board turned over. The people of the town had spoken in that election. There are always teachers and administrators who try and succeed in developing innovative solutions to the issues in our public schools. Our public common schools are alive with innovation and specialty schools.

Charter School Models

The capitalistic form of the charter school model developed in 1991, which was antithetical to Dr. Budde's vision of promoting alternatives within the existing public schools, was the first manifestation of school choice via charters.

The model currently in use is a far cry from the model proposed by Dr. Budde in his book *Charter Schools*. Dr. Budde understood that the charter arrangement could result in a new type of public common school, a type of public common school that Dr. Budde said would give teachers increased responsibility over curriculum and instruction in exchange for a greater degree of accountability for student achievement. It was another choice for parents within the existing public common school district.

Ray Budde's original charter model was district-based and teacher-controlled school choices that parents could opt into. His district model was discarded for a corporate model pushed by the federal government and "choice" advocacy groups at the state level.

As a young undergraduate, the author attended presentations by Dr. Budde. As a superintendent in 1999, the district I led was one of 10 funded with federal Department of Education grants for Public School Choice, the federal effort to jump-start charter schools.

A total of $25 million was available at that time for five-year Public School Choice grants, while at the same time $625 million was made available to privately held charters. This distribution of funds reflects the federal government's efforts to focus on privately held charter schools. This model of federal investment in private schools is currently promoted by the "Freedom Caucus," a front for the Heritage Foundation, which is the major funding source for the conservative caucus and state versions of the conservative caucus.

Charters were a fallback position for these groups as the public overwhelmingly rejected Friedman's voucher model in 1955. The model Friedman proposed for vouchers was developed partially as a response to *Brown v. Board of Education* in 1954 and efforts to desegregate school systems by busing throughout the United States.

- The model has corporate (i.e., an appointed corporate board) rather than local control (i.e., an elected school board).
  - Corporate boards are appointed, not elected. There are no restrictions on who can be appointed.
    - In most cases researched and validated by the Grand Canyon Institute in Arizona, the corporate board is made up of the owners of the corporation, stockholders in for-profit charters, and the owner's relatives.
    - While there may be a "governing board," it is typically made up of employees and members of the corporate board along with the owners.
- The property associated with a charter school is privately held.

- When a charter owner sells his business, there are opportunities to make money on the transfer of real estate to the new owner. This ability to profit applies to for-profit and nonprofit charter properties.
- A typical scenario when this change of hands happens is when the corporation, which was formally for profit, goes nonprofit. The real estate is transferred by the former owner selling it to the new nonprofit, which finances the deal by using bonds that are tax free to the issuers. Millions of dollars transfer to the former charter holder in these cases.
- The newly formed nonprofit now has debt versus the original owner's equity in this property.
- The properties are funded mostly through "junk bonds" sold by hedge funds that profit from the transaction and from the fact that the bonds are tax free at the state and federal level, a form of subsidizing charter borrowing by the federal government.
  - These profits are used by the lenders to pay hedge fund managers and to help corporations finance the election of pro-choice advocates in Congress.
  - These properties are typically overleveraged with high debt loads and little equity.
- Recent federal and state legislative rule changes offer charters "guaranteed loans," putting taxpayers on the hook for loans that are defaulted on. This type of government guaranteed debt was once decried by the Goldwater Institute. They pointed out, correctly, that citizens of the towns taking these loans.[4] They have been silent on the same type of debt assumed by private charter schools and now guaranteed by the state and federal governments. Equally they have been silent regarding the use of PPP funds and ESSER funding during the pandemic by churches, private schools, and charters.

This private ownership model was not the intent of the state laws calling for establishing a public common education in the states. While most public school boards are unpaid members of those boards, many corporate and private school board members receive lucrative payment for service on those corporate boards (in 2019 some board members made in excess of $100,000 as board members) and are often paid employees of the charter, drawing company benefits through related party transactions.

Real Estate Bonanza

In summary, there is a real estate market financing charter schools that looks like the one that went bust in 2008 in the mortgaging of homes that caused a crash that nearly wiped out many banks and bond markets. The bailout of these private companies was engineered by President Obama. The United States recovered most of the bailout funds from reorganized lenders. Some of those same lenders are now in the charter and private school funding game.

- For-profit charter schools do pay property taxes, while nonprofit charter properties are exempt.
  - We expect this to be challenged at some time in the future.
- Churches running private schools are exempt from property taxes on those properties. Local taxes on real estate are the main source of funding for public schools.
- There are many cases when a for-profit charter sells the charter that the new entity creates a nonprofit corporation with the same name. This allows the formerly privately financed property to obtain tax-free bonds to finance the sale and pay off the former property owners (the owner of the charter) with tax-exempt bonds. The new company is then formed as a nonprofit with an undefined owner of the charter (i.e., it is owned by the corporation).
- When a nonprofit charter sells its properties and assets and profits are earned when the property is "refinanced" by the new owners, shouldn't that gain be treated as a capital gain? There is big money being made by management firms that are "leasing" properties to charter schools (their own and others). Imagine Schools, a national charter chain, is noted for using this method.[5]

Traducing Horace Mann and Public Education

In describing Horace Mann's role in the history of public education, the Mackinac Center for Public Policy derisively comments that public schools are "government schools." They go so far as to declare that Horace Mann was "bookish and introspective," as if those qualities constitute a character flaw. Similar left-handed compliments regarding Horace Mann are on other sites extolling the virtues of "choice."

A defining recurring element on these sites is that our current public schools are "government schools" controlled by the state.[6] In fact, the enabling of privately held charter schools and vouchers begins at the federal level and is then acted on at the state level.

Who then are the "government" schools?

An Entitlement Mentality

Education funding at all levels is treated as an entitlement rather than a function of tax-funded efforts to improve the prospects and participation rate in our democratic republic by common citizens of that republic. The reason state and local governments fund public education in a republic is that the republic has a vested interest in literate and intelligent citizens capable of participating in that republic's success. We will demonstrate that data from national sources show that both literacy and high school graduation rates have consistently risen since the advent of public schools in the United States (i.e., the intent of public schools has been realized).

The Founders' Intent

Horace Mann replaced John Quincy Adams in Congress when this great patriot passed away on February 23, 1848. It was John Quincy Adams who argued for the release and return of the slaves aboard the *Amistad* before the Supreme Court in 1839. This was an amazing victory made more amazing by the fact that several of the Court's members were slaveholding southerners.

Horace Mann's respect for the founders' desire to create public common schools in the new republic was deep, influenced by those founders' writings and examples. The story about the establishment of Franklin, Massachusetts, where Horace Mann grew up gives us some idea regarding the influence of one of those founders, Benjamin Franklin, on Horace Mann's thinking and on Franklin's feeling about church and state separation.

A Library Rather than a Church Bell

Franklin, Massachusetts, was established when Franklin separated from Wrentham, Massachusetts, in 1778, and the new town fathers asked Benjamin Franklin to donate a bell to the church in town. Franklin, in a very public way, demurred. Instead he proposed sending a classical library collection to the town that could be lent out to anyone in the area around Franklin, including Wrentham.

"Bookish" Horace Mann, who was born in 1796, read all of those books as part of his self-education process. Mann's determination to keep the educational process out of the hands of an established church are deep and are also founded in his personal experiences and informed by the young republic's desire to keep church and state at arm's length.

Mann's rejection of Calvinism and eventual membership in the Unitarian faith were rooted in his rejection of the type of "New Light" Calvinism that was expounded by Nathanael Emmons, a dominant figure in town politics. In

Mann's own words, Emmons "expounded all the doctrines of total depravity, election, and reprobation, and not only the eternity but the extremity of hell torments, unflinchingly and in their most terrible significance, while he rarely if ever descanted on the joys of heaven, and never, in my recollection, upon the essential and necessary happiness of a virtuous life."

Mann was, by his own account, "a gullible student of such teachings" until the age of fourteen, when his older brother (by four years), Stephen Mann, drowned while swimming in a local lake on a Sunday. Reverend Emmons used the occasion of Stephen's funeral to preach about the hell that awaited those dying in an unconverted state. Hearing his mother's groan of pain at this pronouncement, Mann soon suspended his Calvinist beliefs in a Creator who could be so cruel and commenced his lifelong belief in the kindness and ethical integrity of God.[7] Unitarians of this era believed that they were preserving the essence and values of Christianity, purged of the sectarian and divisive doctrines that divided the Protestant and Roman Catholic faiths. This openness was widespread among the founders despite the refusal of orthodox Calvinists to recognize them as Christians (Barry, 2012). For a modern, well-thought-out take on freedom of religion, Barry's work *Roger Williams and the Creation of the American Soul* is an excellent choice.

Washington, Jefferson, Franklin, Madison, and Monroe were Deists. Deism's philosophical approach is a belief in human reason as the most reliable means of solving the republic's social and political problems.

When he was elected as the first Massachusetts secretary of education in 1837, Horace Mann spearheaded the effort to create common schools throughout Massachusetts. A goal of those common schools was to create locally controlled and governed public schools, where elected board members from the community created policies and procedures that defined what a public common education for all citizens in their communities meant. The idea was not without its detractors then and now. Public common schools were meant to create citizens for the American republic capable of participating in that republic.

Plato's *Republic* spoke of philosopher kings, an educated group that would lead his version of a republic that had free citizens (and was also a slaveholding republic). Plato lived in a time period when there were many gods worshipped by the Greeks. Plato believed in a god that was a transcendent being who used eternal forms to fashion a universe that is eternal and uncreated. Plato's curriculum removed all unseemly stories about the gods. Scholars debate whether he believed in the gods or if the removal was because he felt it was "morally harmful" to the youth of Athens.

The same cast of "conservative" characters that in the 1930s rejected most of Franklin D. Roosevelt's efforts to create a "New Deal" for American citizens living in a republic are now at work trying to decapitate and fragment our system for educating citizens in a republic.

> Democracy cannot succeed unless those who express their choice are prepared to choose wisely. The real safeguard of democracy, therefore, is education.
>
> —Franklin D. Roosevelt

In his book *The Republic and the School: Horace Mann on the Education of Free Men* (1957), Lawrence A. Cremin, America's foremost educational historian and the editor of this reprint of Mann's work, laid out Horace Mann's intentions for public education. Horace Mann's vision, which in no trivial way matched the espoused theories of the founders regarding education as a necessary ingredient in the success of our republic, is clear.

Education as a Moral Enterprise

Cremin's astute editorializing of Mann's ideas for public education summarizes the fact that Mann saw public education as a "moral enterprise." This distinction, calling for a moral enterprise as a function of public education in a republic, is a key part of Mann's argument for public common schools. This central tenet has been critiqued as an "Achilles's heel" of Mann's educational philosophy. It is also one of the reasons why the churches of the time fought against the state creating public common schools. What did Mann mean by his term "moral enterprise"?

The nature of a "moral enterprise" is a subtopic in Cremin's discussion of Mann's legacy.

> Mann understood well the integral relationship between freedom, popular education and republican government. The theme resounds throughout his twelve reports [see Mann's 12 reports to the Massachusetts Board of Education[8]].
>
> A nation cannot long remain ignorant and free. No political structure, however artfully devised, can inherently guarantee the rights and liberties of citizens, for freedom can be secure only as knowledge is widely distributed among the populace. Hence, universal popular education is the only foundation on which republican government can securely rest. These Jeffersonian propositions he accepted as truisms which, by the 1840s, had been voiced so frequently as to be trite. (p. 7)

As a nation, we have strayed from the founders' idealized model for public common education in a democratic republic and adopted instead a mixture of private schools, corporate-owned schools, public schools, and vouchers for private and sectarian schools, an "education model" that is based on a capitalist "business model" advocated by an economist, Milton Friedman. It has been legislated into existence at the federal and state levels through efforts of the private sector and encouraged by "conservative" organizations promoting what is euphemistically termed "school choice." Dr. Budde's model for creating innovative, academically accountable, publicly owned charters has now morphed into vouchers for private sectarian educations with little or no accountability to taxpayers for academic outcomes.

The irony is that this is being done in the name of "freedom of choice."

A major player in this effort to privatize schooling has been ALEC, the American Legislative Exchange Council. ALEC and its supporters advocate for the privatization of most government functions. The reference to "choice" is, of course, to "public" charter schools and the proliferation of private school vouchers (often renamed "opportunity scholarships" prior to a state enacting unlimited vouchers).

We, the American public and our legislators, have allowed ourselves once more to confuse our economic system, capitalism, with our governing system, which is a democratic republic. Public education was never designed to be a purely economic model.

The Logic of Privately Held Publicly Paid For Services Does Not Hold Water

Imagine, if you will, applying the same economic theory to other locally controlled enterprises such as police and fire departments. No one believes that these functions of local government should be private enterprises whose only social responsibility is to the shareholders of the business, a key premise of Milton Friedman's voucher and privatization model.

School choice advocates call public schools "government schools" while endorsing ALEC's "Education Enterprise Zone Act," which allows a state to override a locally elected school board to declare a school "educationally bankrupt." The act diverts public funds to private schools via vouchers. This contradiction is a tell regarding which schools are actually state and federally sponsored schools. This act allows the state to usurp the local governing board in order to enforce "educational enterprise zones." A thorough review of Ronald Reagan's and even Barry Goldwater's writings shows that both of these conservatives knew that local control of schools was an important and vital element of public education. The Freedom Caucus is neither free nor a real caucus. In fact, this group wants freedom to do what they deem is correct and moral and makes political moves to stifle the will of the electorate and individuals.

Conflicts of Interest

Chambers of Commerce, which are private organizations, in our states have supported and endorsed the idea of tax credits (as opposed to tax deductions) for businesses that donate to private scholarship funds (aka "opportunity scholarships"). This effectively removes these sources of income from the funding available to public schools (including "public" charters). In the meantime, it creates "opportunities" for the people running the scholarship funds to profit from the movement of money from donations to the distribution process. We have an idea who this profits. In one state, Arizona, these funds are often controlled by former legislators who are now in the "scholarship" businesses that they established when the "law" went into effect.

Who Is Choosing and Who Is Losing?

The data on STOs from 2022 show that the majority of the funding from these scholarships is going to private sectarian schools.

As of July 2023, an estimate of students in the new (September 2023) unlimited voucher program in Arizona is currently on pace to exceed the budgeted amount for this program. There are currently 746 private schools in Arizona; not all of them took public funding from the parents choosing those schools. The largest increase in spending has been to preschool programs in the state from parents seeking these services for their children.

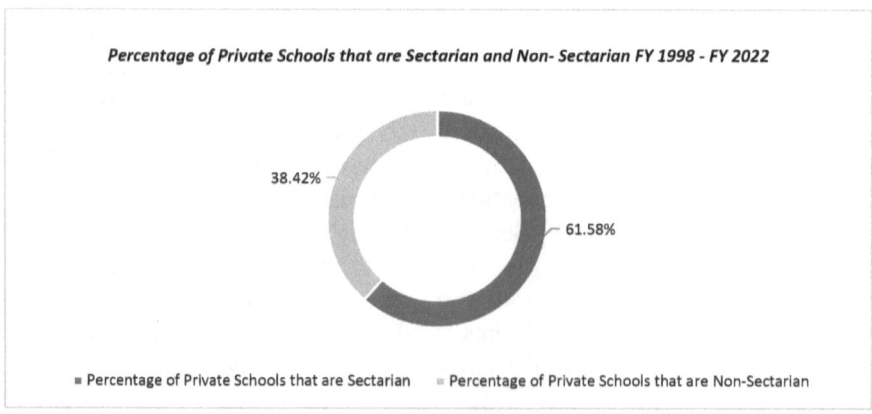

Figure 4.1. Percentage of Private Schools That Are Sectarian and Nonsectarian, FY 2022
Source: Arizona Department of Revenue reports, collated by Grand Canyon Institute.

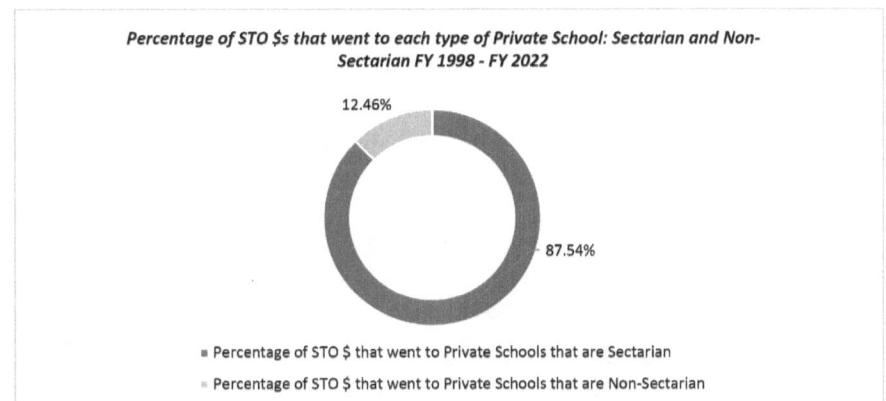

Figure 4.2. Percentage of STO Funds Going to Sectarian Schools
Source: Arizona Department of Revenue report for FY 2022, analysis by Grand Canyon Institute.

Table 4.1. Distributions of STO Funds in Arizona, FY 1998–FY 2022

Nonsectarian private schools	$249,318,390
Catholic private schools	$916,577,316
Christian (non-Catholic) private schools	$719,890,833
Jewish private schools	$91,608,901
Islamic private schools	$22,876,088
Total	**$2,000,271,528**

Source: Arizona Department of Revenue report for FY 2022, analysis by Grand Canyon Institute.

How Did We Fall for This Attack on Our Public School System?

We can date the movement to offer school choice to the Supreme Court's decisions regarding prayer in school and *Brown v. Board of Education*. In his book *Market Education: The Untold Story* (1999), Andrew Coulson, who is one of the prime proponents of moving back to a market-based educational system, traces that model back in time. His writings have influenced the privatization movement, but by far the greatest influencer in the concept of market-based education was Milton Friedman.

Evaluating the impact on state spending is often discussed as simple math (e.g., the typical cost for a public school education is $14,000; therefore, spending 90% of the charter rate of $8,800 on vouchers saves money). A similar argument was used to advocate for charters.

The logic holds somewhat true for state spending on education, but as Figure 4.3 illustrates, this mainly affects the use of state funding.

Defenders of the voucher model call it common sense that vouchers save money.

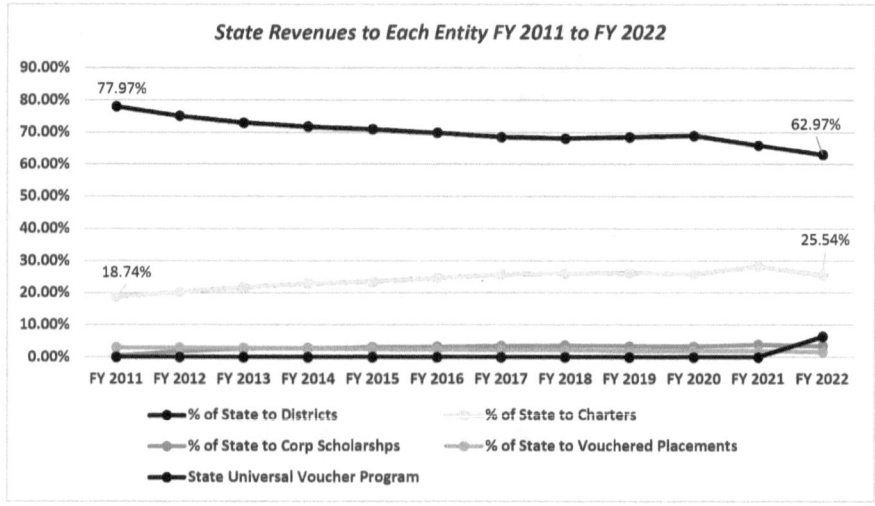

Figure 4.3. State Spending in Each Category of Publicly Funded Education
Source: Arizona Department of Revenue report for FY 2022 and data from the superintendent's annual report, analysis by Grand Canyon Institute.

Here is a commonsense way, in simple math with traditional characters in an equation, to really simplify the math.

Common Sense Using Simple Math

With apologies to Dick and Jane.

Jane Hidalgo, Dick McPherson, and Frank Emerson have children in K–12 education in Arizona.

All three of their family units make an income that is three times above the poverty level for a family of four.

All three have no children in a special education placement.

All three live in the same town with a low property tax rate and a large tax base.

Jane sends her three children to three different Arizona public schools; two attend the high school in a neighboring town for sports reasons.

- Jane uses public schools within and outside her district using Arizona's open enrollment rules.
- Dick sends his children to a Christian private school in the town next to the one he lives in. He used to pay for this himself; now he is using the new state voucher program.
- Frank sends his three children to a charter school.

What This Used to Cost the State of Arizona

Simple math: The state of Arizona prior to vouchers but with school choice at charters was already spending:

- $7,500 for Jane's children (rate of $2,500 per child from equalization funding).
- $0 for Dick's children. Dick paid full tuition for all three.
- $24,600 for Frank's children (rate of $8,800 per charter student).
- Total cost to state revenues: **$32,100**.

What the State of Arizona Is Now Funding After Universal Vouchers

New state costs associated with these post-voucher choices:

- $7,500 for Jane's children.
- $26,400 for Dick's children in their Christian school private placements, leaving Dick with the balance on the tuition cost, which, surprise, the private school raised when vouchers became available.
- $24,600 for Frank's children in their charter school placements.
- Total cost to state revenues for education: **$58,500**.

Question: Which is the larger number, $32,000 or $58,500? Use scratch paper if you need to and show your work.

Extra Credit

In FY 2020, there were 5.72 million private school students in the United States.

In 2023, there were 69,341 private school students in Arizona.

That same year there were 50.8 million public and charter students in the United States.

What would the cost to the states be from adding 5.72 million students at $8,000 (on average?

On August 24, Tom Horne, the Republican superintendent of public instruction in Arizona, began a series of advertisements which he claims are aimed at poorer voters wishing to use the Empowerment Scholarship Accounts (ESA) program (unlimited vouchers). The ads were funded by a slush fund given to the Arizona legislature to do with as they saw fit.

Tom Horne is supposed to be the superintendent of public instruction. Private schools are not public instruction; district schools and charters, using the language of the legislature, are public schools. We only own one type of these public schools.

Socioeconomic Question

The average cost for private schools in the United States was $12,350 per student in FY 2020.

Explain how a lower-income family (earning less than three times the poverty rate) could now afford to send their child to a private school with their limited voucher funds.

Who Do We Choose to Follow the Lead Of?

Do we follow the lead of Horace Mann, who said, "Be ashamed to die until you have won some small victory for mankind," or Friedman's market model that insists, "The only moral obligation of a business is to make money for its stockholders"? What kind of a moral educational choice is that?

One is the path of hope for all citizens of our republic, the other a method for enriching private corporations, religions, and private schools with taxpayer resources. One is locally controlled, the other privately held by corporations and churches. The old arguments concerning bureaucrats running our public schools pale when one considers mega-charters with tens of thousands of students in multiple states and church schools beholden to the hierarchies of those religions.

We have been here before. The majority clearly chose locally controlled public education. The same majority of the population spoke up and said they did not support defunding or privatization of the police during our issues with policing.

We do not want to privatize our military. When we hire private firms to provide military-type services, the costs often exceed $1,000 per day for each of the employees of those mercenary services. This cost does not include overhead or management fees.

Giving up ownership of our schools and paying for educational services deprives the public of the ownership of the schools it is funding. These are school sites that we rely on during emergencies to house those who have lost their homes, where we gather in a public place to console our towns in time of loss, and that we call the home team.

It is not only bad policy for publicly paid for real estate. It is a poor economic choice.

NOTES

1. https://www.whitehousehistory.org/the-pearl-incident
2. The term "rule of thumb" comes from the colonial-era law that said you could beat your wife, servants, and children with a rod that was as wide as your thumb.
3. https://www.nytimes.com/2005/06/21/us/ray-budde-82-first-to-propose-charter-schools-dies.html
4. Debt and Taxes: Arizona Taxpayers on Hook for $66 Billion Tab Run Up by State, Local Governments (goldwaterinstitute.org)
5. See "How Tax Exempt Are Charter Schools on Land Owned by For-Profit Investors," https://nonprofitquarterly.org/how-tax-exempt-are-charter-schools-on-land-owned-by-for-profit-investors
6. https://www.mackinac.org/2035
7. https://uudb.org/articles/horacemann.html
8. https://college.cengage.com/history/ayers_primary_sources/massachusetts_board_education_1840.htm

REFERENCES

Barry, J. M. (2012). *Roger Williams and the creation of the American soul: Church, state, and the birth of liberty*. New York: Viking.

Coulson, A. J. (1999). *Market education: The unknown history*. New Brunswick, NJ: Transaction Publishers.

Tharp, L. H. (1953). *Until victory: Horace Mann and Mary Peabody*. Boston: Little, Brown.

Chapter 5

Paying for Public Common Schools

That such education should be paid for, controlled, and sustained by an interested public

—Horace Mann

LOCAL CONTROL: LOCAL OWNERSHIP

Local districts used to be more plentiful. What was preserved during some of the consolidation of districts into "school administrative unions" and larger districts was control by the local school board(s) of its own budget, curriculum, and school properties within those districts. That is, the management at the district level did not usurp local control. People have been led to believe the bureaucratic lie regarding superintendents and district offices. A superintendent is an agent of the board, not the director of that board. Their placement at a board meeting is usually to one side of the board with the board chair in the center seat. This fact is often ignored in discussions regarding large school districts (i.e., control of the local district's real estate did not necessarily move up to the management level at the superintendent's office). Consolidation of districts was occurring when Milton Friedman first wrote his thesis regarding "bureaucracies" at large school districts.

Charters have their own issues with size. Their management costs are often a larger percentage of expenditures than those of districts, even though they often count administration costs (i.e., the 2,400 accounts regarding school building administration) in a different manner, categorizing this under instructional costs. Many private schools are run by church hierarchies (bureaucracies by another name) beholden to church leadership for guidance in how to operate their schools. In Arizona alone, the fund-raising arm of the Catholic diocese has three employees making a total of over $300,000.[1]

Who Has the Real Bureaucratic Organization?

One of Milton Friedman's complaints regarding school districts was that they had become too large (i.e., they had become bureaucracies). The rise of large school districts can have that effect if their boards allow it. However, the same issues can affect mega-charter organizations, which have more than 10,000 students and may have schools in multiple states. Data also show that on average, charter administrative spending is twice as much as local school district spending for the same administrative services (see Figure 5.1).

For-Profit Management Corporations

Charters using for-profit charter management corporations to operate central office services are even more expensive, with many management fees that are over 25% of the total budget for the charter.[2] In addition, most of the largest charter corporations have a presence in multiple states and are expanding at a rapid rate. These organizations often "lease" the teachers of their schools, making that expense a "purchased service." Some even charge a premium for this service. What is clear in any of these arrangements for hiring and paying staff is that the public does not pay the staff; the corporation does (i.e., the teachers and administrators are not public employees). Often the management company, which often has a different name than the schools, owns the buildings and property and "leases" them to the school.

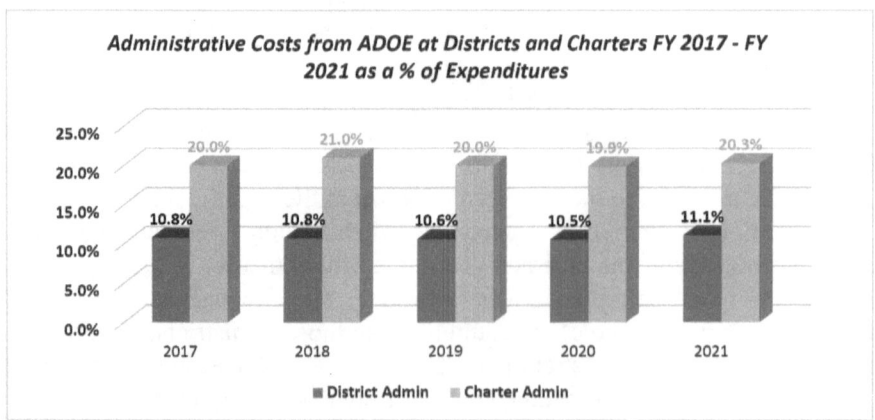

Figure 5.1. Administrative Costs at Arizona Districts and Charters
Source: Arizona superintendents' annual reports, FY 2017–FY 2022, analysis by Grand Canyon Institute.

Charter funding, scholarship fund dollars, and voucher funding come almost exclusively from the state and federal government either directly or indirectly (scholarship fund dollars are credited "donations" that come off the donor business's state taxes on a one-to-one basis).

This begs the question, "Who are the 'government' schools in this equation?" As mentioned in a prior chapter, the author was there at the inception of charter school grants from the U.S. Department of Education,[3] which as of this date has spent $4 billion promoting what is euphemistically referred to as "innovation and improvement." Most of these "grants" pass through the states' charter school funding. Charters also benefited from the PPP program and federal loan programs (ESSER 1 and 2).[4] They are also collecting money for special-needs children, Title 1, and federal food programs. Lawmakers in Washington work to make these federal dollars flow to their states. There is even a congressional caucus on Education Innovation and Opportunity.[5] Funding of charter properties is also conducted by the USDA under its rural grants programs.

The range of Figures 5.2 and 5.3 depicting where each type of school is receiving funding from includes the year 2021. Without the infusion of federal PPP loans and ESSER 1 and 2 loans (forgivable), charters would have suffered unsustainable losses during FY 2021 and FY 2022. When the ESSER loans were removed from the revenue statements, the Grand Canyon Institute found that 127 of 424 charter corporations would have ended the year with catastrophic losses. During this four-year span of time, 44 charter sites closed while the largest charter corporations (top 20 of 240 corporations) increased their percentage of student attendance (average daily membership, ADM). The percentage of revenue from the federal programs that year was up 100% from prior years, mainly through those programs. At districts, the percentage

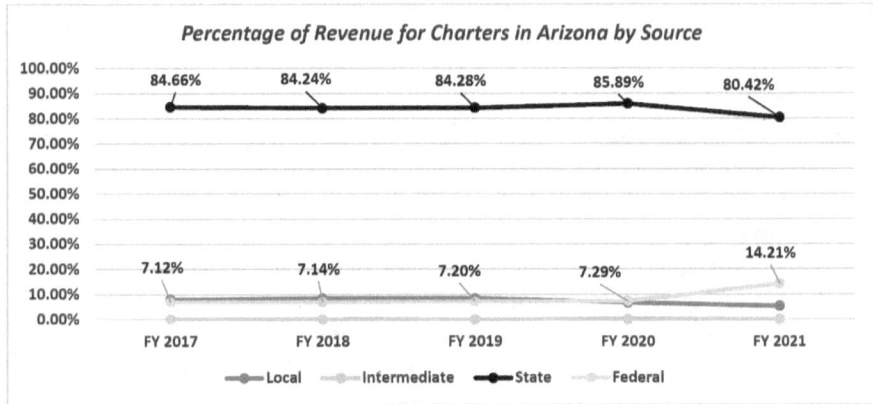

Figure 5.2. Revenue Sources at Arizona Charters

Source: Arizona superintendents' annual reports, FY 2017–FY 2022, analysis by Grand Canyon Institute.

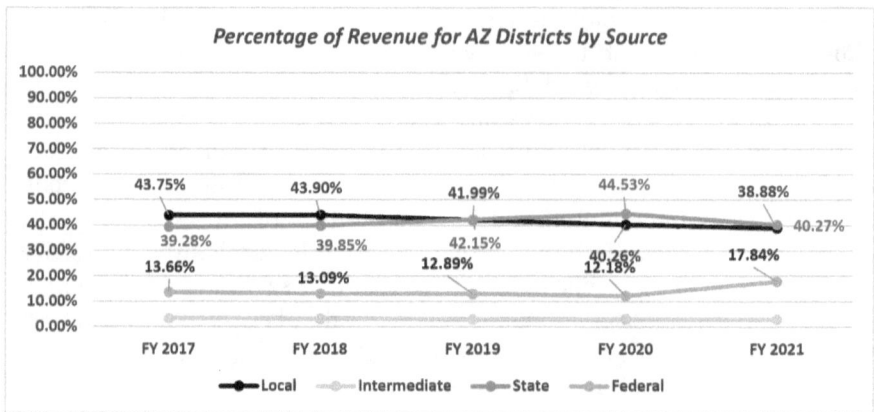

Figure 5.3. Revenue Sources at Arizona Districts
Source: Arizona superintendent's annual report, FY 2017–FY 2021, analysis by Grand Canyon Institute.

went up 50% from prior years. Clearly, charter schools, through the efforts of their supporters in Congress, were major beneficiaries from this federal largesse. The point is that "free markets" were again impinged upon at this time by direct federal intervention into the education marketplace via PPP and ESSER funds.

Federal and State Loan Guarantees to Private Corporations

During Betsy DeVos's tenure as U.S. secretary of education, the federal and state governments began a program of guaranteeing loans (IDA tax-free bonds) for charter schools. Considering the fact that there is a 38% failure rate at charter schools, it is readily apparent that without federal and state financial intervention via guaranteed and tax-free bonding through IDA, there would be greater asset losses at charter schools. In the meantime, district bond issues to accommodate growth at the locally owned and paid for schools have been voted down by citizens no longer vested in their local schools. Public apathy is directed at schools that the public actually owns and that manage that financial support well (districts typically have a .2 to .3 debt-to-asset ratio, which is excellent).

Charter advocates insist that a constant debt load is what their market anticipated, as well as losses due to charter schools' failures to attract students. The implication is that the losses must have occurred because of mismanagement or poor academic performance. These arguments do not hold up. Charters have debt loads that are on average two times the amounts held by districts per student. This means that large amounts of their expenditures are being used to pay debt and interest rather than to educate children. State IDA loans, which are tax free at the state and federal level, reward this restructuring of debt to assets, which is continuous. The real beneficiaries are the bond markets.

By any measure, the charter industry, and most likely private schools, is overleveraged.

Leveraging Debt to Pay for Real Estate Investment

When a charter owner sells to a new owner or to the remaining organization, the organization allows that owner to "cash out" their equity and refinance the properties held by the charter group. Payouts in the millions are typical. Exaggerated claims of "goodwill" on balance sheets provide fodder for inflated sale prices. For-profit charters often convert to "nonprofit" when this occurs, as the "for-profit" owner may have made a real estate investment at the outset of the charter's existence at his or her own risk. Converting the charter to nonprofit status allows the recreated charter to obtain federal and state tax-exempt IDA loans to "purchase" the property from the former for-profit owners. These sales are legal and not frowned upon by the organizations overseeing the charters (e.g., the state board for charter schools).

In FY 2018, the Arizona State Board for Charter Schools (ASBCS) sought and received permission to close charters for financial issues. They have cut the number of charters closing during the school year to zero by monitoring the finances of each charter for ADM loss and other factors. The ASBCS takes its charge seriously and does an excellent job monitoring audits and performance.

Private schools and voucher users have no such oversight board. In the case of vouchers, the preferred method of tracking is a program created by a privatization entrepreneur, "ClassWallet." In Arizona, a major data breach of that system was discovered that allowed personal information and special education information to be tapped into. Just like the oft-criticized welfare debit cards, the rate of abuse and self-serving payments (i.e., payments to yourself through a third party for "guiding" your own children through a micro-school) is around 10%.

The Debt Time Bomb in Charter Finances

This debt load creates a new burden for the nonprofit charter. Paying debt that is equal to your equity is never a good financial plan. Carrying that debt on a publicly funded enterprise (and recently, newly guaranteed loans by the federal and state government) leaves taxpayers on the hook for private debts. Junk bond and hedge fund companies make the lion's share of the profits from this "tax-free" bond market. It is one reason why those firms are so supportive of "choice" and politicians who are in the pocket of the charter school industry and the junk bond dealers benefiting from long-term debt at charters.

Debt-to-Asset Ratios

A standard measure of a business's financial position is the company's debt-to-asset ratio. An analysis of the years from FY 2014 through FY 2022 yields the data depicted in Figure 5.6.

The Threat to Public Properties

Charter and private school advocates insist that they should be able to take over sites that a school district has closed due to loss of students. Some states have written this expectation into their charter legislation.

As a consumer of educational services, which is how charters and private schools see their clients, which firms look like they are more likely to collapse from a debt-to-asset ratio that is greater than .6? Even from a pure capitalist business point of view, this imbalance in debt to assets is beyond the scope of financial best practices.

Despite Milton Friedman's and the school choice advocates' arguments, there is no question that "paid for, controlled, and sustained by an interested public" are not elements of either charter schools or privately held schools'

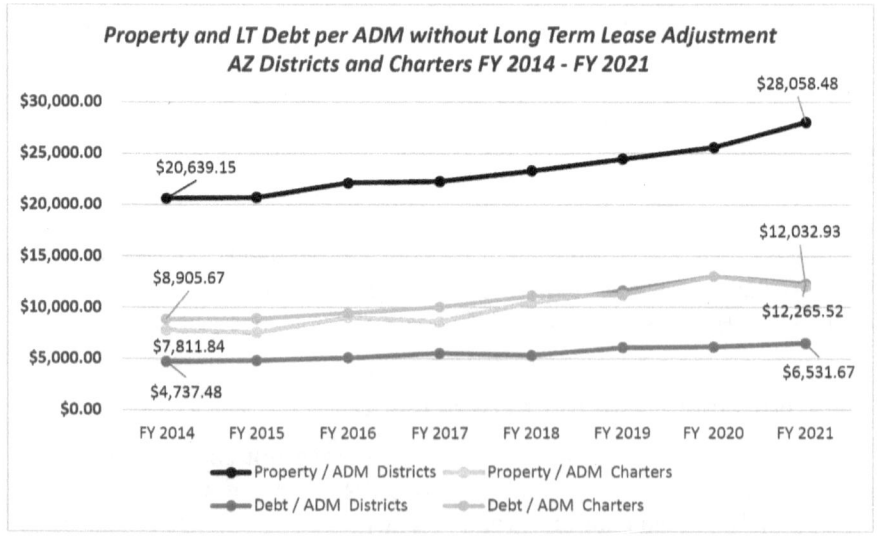

Figure 5.4. Comparison of Debt per ADM at Arizona Charters and School Districts
Source: Arizona superintendents' annual reports, FY 2014–FY 2021, analysis by Grand Canyon Institute.

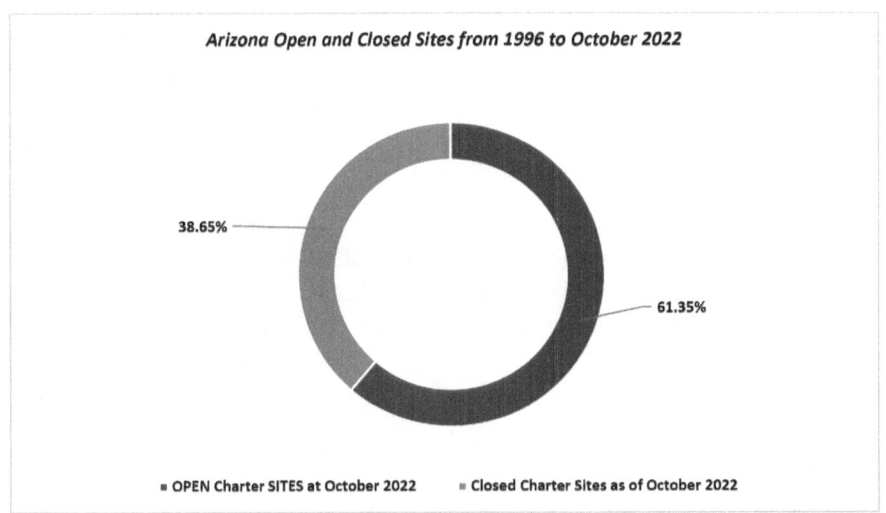

Figure 5.5. Failure Rate of Arizona Charter Sites
Source: Analysis of ASBCS data on site closures without counting charter sites that merged with another site.

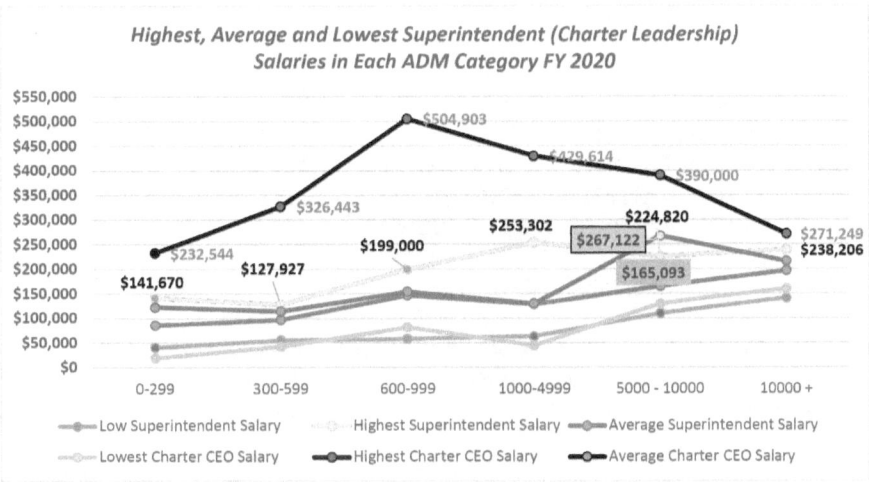

Figure 5.6. Highest, Average, and Lowest Managerial Salaries at Arizona Charters and Districts by Organization Size
Source: Survey of superintendents' salaries by Grand Canyon Institute, FY 2020, and IRS 990 data for charter salaries.

voucher choices. Recently enacted "voucher expansions," which benefit (85%) people from high-income zip codes who were already paying for their "choice," now subsidize partially paid for rides to private and sectarian schools. These "choosers" already choose to pay for their child's private education and can afford the difference between the voucher cost and tuition, which can be twice as much.

Who Is in Control at a Private Sectarian Voucher Paid For School?

Catholic schools, as an example, are controlled by the diocese (i.e., the bishop of the diocese or archdiocese). Typical policy reads like the following (note: the capitalization in this policy is in the original document):

Policy 3–1 Catholic Schools

The following policies and procedures are established by the Diocese to assist the Superintendent of Schools (in the case of a Diocesan School), the Pastor (in the case of a Parish School) and Principals and Preschool Directors in the administration of Catholic schools in the Diocese.

3-1.1 ADMINISTRATION

3-1.1.01 THE ROLE OF THE BISHOP

THE BISHOP HAS FULL RESPONSIBILITY FOR THE EDUCATIONAL MINISTRIES OF THE DIOCESE OF PHOENIX. ALL POLICIES INCLUDED IN THIS DIOCESAN HANDBOOK OF POLICIES, PROCEDURES AND NORMS FOR CATHOLIC SCHOOLS (HEREINAFTER, "HANDBOOK") HAVE BEEN APPROVED BY THE BISHOP.

Relevant Canons from the Code of Canon Law

Canon 794 §1. The duty and right of educating belongs in a special way to the Church,[6] to which has been divinely entrusted the mission of assisting persons so that they are able to reach the fullness of the Christian life.

§2. Pastors of souls have the duty of arranging everything so that all the faithful have a Catholic education.

Canons 803–806 are specifically applicable to the Bishop's oversight role in Catholic Schools.

Canon 803 §1. A Catholic school is understood as one which a competent ecclesiastical authority or a public ecclesiastical juridical person directs or which ecclesiastical authority recognizes as such through a written document.

§2. The instruction and education in a Catholic school must be grounded in the principles of Catholic doctrine; teachers are to be outstanding in correct doctrine and integrity of life.

§3. Even if it is in fact Catholic, no school is to bear the name Catholic school without the consent of competent ecclesiastical authority.[7]

As noted, the author and his brothers were all sent to Catholic school from grade 1 through high school. Our parents paid for that free choice and our indoctrination into the Catholic Church. The education at our local public schools was more comprehensive, and they actually taught science, which didn't occur in our diocese elementary schools until we were in eighth grade (in 1966).

At one point, while Horace Mann was still living, the pope declared that anyone who lived in an area with a Catholic school must send their children to that school under penalty of mortal sin. This was at a time when *McGuffey's Reader* had blatantly anti-Catholic readings in its books. The Catholic Church opposed the establishment of public schools, claiming that the education of Catholics was a function of the church, not the state or local government.[8]

Boards of Directors Versus School Boards

Charter schools have corporate boards that are supposed to oversee the charter and ensure that the charter holder is running the company in a way that is consistent with its educational mission statements. The owner is not an agent of the board like a superintendent in a school district is. The board members at a charter can be and often are the owner and members of his or her family. School board members at public districts are typically unpaid, elected positions. Nepotistic policies are strong in our districts.

Corporate board members may be and often are compensated for their roles. In the research done for this book, the author came across several corporate board members being paid for their board membership at multiple charters. Cross-referencing the data shows that several key members of one charter are allowed to be on the boards of competing charters (i.e., there are no conflict-of-interest barriers). Board members at private and charter schools may also have related-party transactions with their schools.

In the case of sectarian schools, the school can be, and is, a revenue source for the church. Considering that churches believe that tithing is a function of membership in the church (10% of the congregant's gross salary in religions that tithe) and that they preach to their congregations regarding where their faithful should attend school, one wonders why they are still tax-exempt organizations.

The data show multiple charters owned by pastors at churches. Those full-time pastors then draw their salary from the school organization as full-time presidents and vice presidents of the attached charter school. These are often husband-and-wife teams. One such team of pastors took over $392,000 in salaries for a school with a student population of 1,590 in FY 2019. The school property is owned by the church. There is no evidence (i.e., a separate IRS 990 nonprofit filing) that the pastors (listed as president and vice president of the charter corporation) are paid anything directly from the church operations. The organization refused a request to provide separate accounting for the church that owns the charter school. The financial evidence appears to show that there is only one entity controlling the charter and the church.

The argument for these arrangements is that often husband-and-wife teams save the school money. In some cases this is true. Data on this subject gleaned from IRS 990s show this to be the case in schools with populations under 199 students; however, once the number climbs to the next range of sizes, another pattern emerges. A comparison of salaries of top management at charters and district superintendents shows that there is indeed money to be made as a charter holder.

Board policies at public schools do not allow board members to benefit financially from their relationship with the school district. That is one of the key elements of local, elected oversight of the schools. Superintendent salaries are negotiated by the board, as are benefits for this position. Justifications for large salaries at charters say things like, "The board looked at the marketplace when determining compensation for the leaders of the charter." This is true for marketplace positions for CEOs, not in school districts. There are

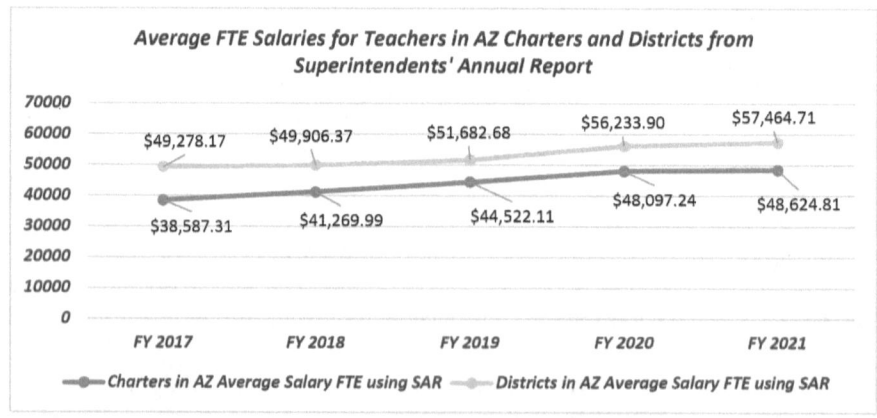

Figure 5.7. Teacher Salary Averages at Arizona Charters and Districts
Source: Arizona superintendents' annual reports, FY 2017–FY 2021.

"for-profit" owners who took $10 million and more in compensation for the year as a "distribution" to the owners (i.e., the charter holders).

Critics of public schools have always complained about superintendent salaries despite numerous studies showing that there is little to no correlation between what superintendents make and what teachers make. The argument put forth is that teachers could make more if administrators did not make so much. Simple mathematics dispel this notion (i.e., a superintendent's salary divided by all teaching staff adding to their salaries is a small amount). Left out of these discussions is the fact that small districts often pay a small stipend to their superintendent who is also working in another administrative role. Similarly, small charters are less likely to pay a large salary to the owner or the "superintendent."

Another argument for "choice" has been that once freed from unions, teachers would earn what they are worth. At the time this was written, Friedman claimed that teachers would make $100,000 once the market set their value (1975).

What Happened to That Claim?

When Dr. Budde of the University of Massachusetts proposed the concept of chartering schools, the charters he described were funded and controlled by the local school board. Teachers would be in charge of these schools and covered under collective bargaining agreements. As leaders in their charter schools, teachers could make more money for taking on this role. His idea was taken and turned into the free market, corporate-driven model that constitutes today's charter industry, an industry where teachers are underpaid and have limited benefit packages. A look at a comparison of salaries tells one side of how that played out for teachers (see Figure 5.8). The other tell in the data is benefits (see Figure 5.9). In a free market, this is called controlling labor costs.

To their credit, some states establish rules allowing charter teachers to participate in the state's retirement plan. This is questionable, as they are not state or local employees but employees of the corporation. Even so, disappointingly, only 38.5% of charters participate. Of that 38.5%, there are four charter corporations that only participate at the managerial level. This is allowed because those companies "lease" their teachers using a related teacher-leasing entity managed by their management group. This makes those teachers ineligible for the retirement system while management keeps its status as eligible. Since the inception of charters, several of the larger charters that started as participants in the retirement system have dropped out, sometimes after the top personnel had gained enough points to collect a full pension. This gaming of the retirement system designed to protect teachers in

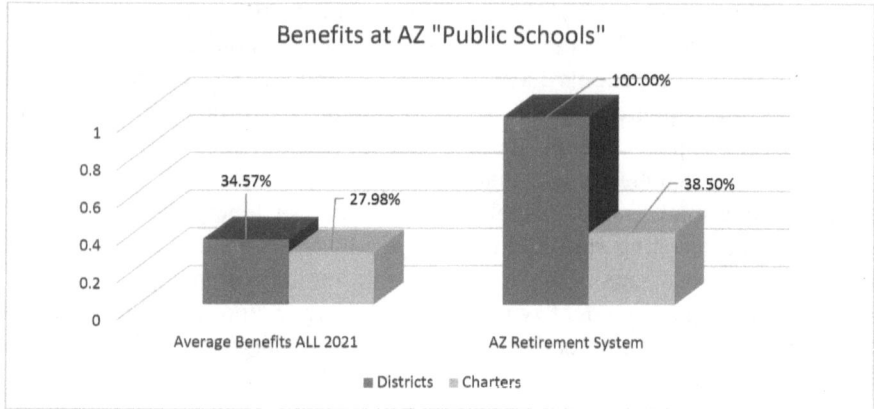

Figure 5.8. Average Benefits at Arizona Charters and Districts
Source: Arizona superintendents' annual reports, FY 2017–FY 2021.

their golden years continues. Gaming like this also jeopardizes the financial position of state retirement systems.

Matching Retirement Contributions

When we read that companies have a matching plan for retirement that includes a match of 4% and then do the math concerning the amount put into this fund as reported on the audits, we find that the average in these plans is 1.25% of the payroll. This is one of the reasons that the first step in the choice process is for the states to become "right to work" states where union membership is not allowed to be a condition of employment. When questioned about this, one large firm responded that they only expect their teachers to be employees for three years and that retirement systems cost these teachers without the benefit of a return on that investment as they are not vested in three years. Vested means you can leave and take the funds you paid into the state's retirement system.

Locally Controlled Schools Are Serious About Stemming the Turnover Rate in the Teaching Profession

Local control by school boards leads communities to value their teachers and commit to their long-term employment in the town that they elect to become a vital part of. Dr. Budde, whom I listened to and read as an undergraduate at the University of Massachusetts at Salem in 1973, understood this.[9]

Charter schools as they currently exist and vouchers for private schools do not fit Horace Mann's principle "that such education should be paid for, controlled, and sustained by an interested public."

Private enterprises controlling public education expenditures is anathema to the intent of the founders and a prime example of the folly of market-based education models foisted on the public by those wishing to capitalize on publicly funded education. The public is being forced to subsidize religious, private educational choices.

What is next in a capitalistic system? If I don't use public parks, do I get a voucher for my country club membership equal to the amount per citizen spent on those public parks? Paid-for choice is a slippery slope if responsibility for that choice's costs is left out of the equation.

NOTES

1. Arizona Department of Revenue annual report on expenditures at STOs, FY.
2. There are two examples in Arizona where over 90% of the budget is identified as management (2300 and 2500 account codes).
3. https://www2.ed.gov/about/offices/list/oii/csp/grants.html
4. https://www.azed.gov/esser-i-ii
5. https://www.legistorm.com/organization/summary/123129/Congressional_Caucus_on_Education_Innovation_and_Opportunity.html
6. This control issue has always been a factor in the Catholic Church's opposition to public schools dating back to the first common school laws in Massachusetts. Similar types of control issues (i.e., who should control education) were common with many of the churches operating in Massachusetts when Horace Mann was in charge of public education.
7. http://dphx.org/wp-content/uploads/2016/01/Policy-3-1.1-Administration.pdf
8. https://www.educationnext.org/politics-choice-when-public-school-was-born-review-public-vs-private-robert-n-gross provides an argument supporting the church's position and claiming that the motivating factor for public schools was a fear of "popery."
9. https://files.eric.ed.gov/fulltext/ED605247.pdf

Chapter 6

"That This Education Must Be Nonsectarian"

WHO IS IN CONTROL AT A PRIVATE SECTARIAN VOUCHER- OR SCHOLARSHIP-ACCEPTING SCHOOL?

Vouchers and opportunity scholarships are often touted as a way to provide choice to special-needs children, veterans' children, people who live in poverty, and other special groups of students. In fact, the vast majority of these funds go to sectarian "choices" for a religious education. Additionally, vouchers are mainly used by people who are above three times the poverty rate for a family of four. States like New Hampshire have at least made income considerations a part of their voucher program.

The public is forced to assist in the payment of tuition by the commandeering of our tax revenues via tax credits to donors to these funds or by the state legislature through voucher expansions. Either way, these policies support the sectarian choices of individual citizens as if a type of "publicly paid for" education is a right, not a privilege. The right to an education was improperly and wrongly pronounced in the *Wall Street Journal*'s April 29, 2006, front-page headline, "The Constitution Guarantees a Public-School K–12 Education for Every Child in the U.S." That headline is what the average person seeking payment for their private choices (including homeschool) believes, as they have been lied to so many times that they are militant regarding their "choice." This includes using a micro-school and paying themselves as the guide for leading their homeschooled child's online program.

The Cato Institute refuted this statement in an editorial the *Wall Street Journal* published later in the week declaring that the federal government should "enforce" No Child Left Behind's mandates. CATO reminded the *Journal* that education is not mentioned in the Constitution of the United

States for a reason. That reason is clearly stated: "The Founders wanted most aspects of life managed by those who were closest to the people, local government. Certainly, the founders saw no role for the federal government in education."[1]

This statement also speaks to the fact that the Tenth Amendment left unstated governance issues to the states and the people. The establishment clause was meant to define the separation of government from religious interference or as a test for public office. As Jefferson said, the wall of separation is there to protect religion.

The argument that vouchers are not a direct support by the state because the parents made the "choice" and the ClassWallet program where state funds are taken care of is used as an intermediary step to getting at those funds, doesn't alter the fact that public funds are going to support sectarian schools.

The state pretends that they are allowing parents a choice they already had, except that now they, the parents, can obtain funding that they have an entitlement to thanks to the legislature. Usually the amounts have some connection to what is spent by the state at district schools or charters, but the inferences made always cite the district averages, which of course include local taxpayer funds which those advocating for vouchers and choice often claim are also part of their entitlement.

The U.S. Supreme Court at the time when this issue was hotly contested (1943) had also refused to recognize any right to a taxpayer-funded education. As Timothy Sandefur, in his book *Cornerstone of Liberty: Property Rights in 21st-Century America*, points out, in *San Antonio Independent School District v. Rodriguez* (1973), the Court specifically declared that education, though important, "is not among the rights afforded explicit protection under our Federal Constitution. Nor do we find any basis for saying it is implicitly so protected." Nine years later, in *Plyler v. Doe*, the Court held that *if* a state chooses to give such an education to citizens, it must also offer it to the children of illegal aliens. But it has consistently recognized that taxpayer-funded education is a privilege, not a right.[2] The first attempts to establish vouchers in various states are typically pushed back on and denied by the voters. An end run around this opposition attempts to sidestep it by offering opportunity scholarships run by STOs that spring up to collect "tax-credit donations" from businesses to fund this type of program in place of vouchers. Experience shows that the next step is universal vouchers, as in Florida and Arizona. Since the Supreme Court cases noted earlier, this has changed dramatically. The floodgates have been opened.

Arizona has a history of tax-credit-funded opportunity scholarships, and as of FY 2023 it has the nation's most expansive voucher program. Who is choosing these scholarships?

At the end of FY 2021, the data presented in Table 6.1 were reported.[3] The Grand Canyon Institute collated these data from the less than 30% of all expenditures that went to nonsectarian schools. The fact that "Christian" and "Catholic" schools identify themselves as such (they are both Christian) should be an alarm as to what is promulgated at these schools (i.e., are Catholics not Christians?). Another five schools listed as Islamic benefited from these STOs.

These groups, as we noted in the prior chapter, have their own rules as to who controls the schools and what is taught. In addition, private schools are the owners of those school assets, not the public being asked to participate in these new universal voucher programs. The sectarian issue is not only present in the scholarship and voucher programs; there are sectarian charters operating under the guise of "nonsectarian" Christian schools. In June 2023, Oklahoma's charter board accepted a charter for an online Catholic school. This "choice" is working its way through legal challenges.

In addition to this, STOs are allowed to have paid contractors or their own hired employees for the purpose of fund-raising on their behalf. One such group, the Christian Scholarship Fund, was immediately set up by the former head of the state legislature and is currently run by paid family members. The organization rents space from the former legislature. In addition, the funds can carry over (up to 10%) from year to year. In FY 2022, there were 33,806 scholarships taken that totaled over $66 million. As Table 6.2 shows, the STOs kept another $28.5 million in reserves that year. The average scholarship was $2,755.

Sectarian Charters Posing as Public Charters

The governance of public school districts is local and controlled by an elected board.

Charter schools have corporate boards that are supposed to oversee the charter and ensure that the charter holder is running the company in a way

Table 6.1. Sectarian and Nonsectarian Beneficiaries of STOs

Total	Christian	Catholic	Jewish	Private Nonsectarian
252	112	58	8	74
Percentage	Christian	Catholic	Jewish	Private Nonsectarian
	44.44%	23.02%	3.17%	29.37%
Percentage		Christian and Catholic	Jewish	Private Nonsectarian
		67.46%	3.17%	29.37%

Source: Arizona Department of Revenue report on STOs FY 2022, collated by Grand Canyon Institute.

Table 6.2. STO Overall Data for FY 2022

Number of Scholarships	Total Scholarships Paid Out	Average Scholarships	Number of Schools	Number of Future Reserved	Amount Reserved
33,806	$66,066,989	$2,755	1,242	12,477	$28,501,272

Source: Arizona Department of Revenue report for FY 2022, collated by author.

that is consistent with its educational mission statements. The owner is not an agent of the board like a superintendent in a school district is (i.e., there is really no check on decisions made by management). In the case of sectarian schools, the school can be, and is, a revenue source for the church sponsoring the school. Considering that churches believe that tithing is a function of membership in the church (10% of the congregant's gross salary) and that they preach to their congregations regarding where their "faithful" should attend school, one wonders why they are still tax-exempt organizations since they are drawing on tax revenues for their enterprises. These organizations are even ignoring the Bible's admonition to render to Caesar that which is Caesar's and to God that which is God's, taking funds from our state's coffers to run their sectarian schools.

Paying the Clergy From the State's Largesse

Data gleaned from IRS 990 filings show multiple charters owned by pastors at churches that draw their salary from the school organization. These, as noted earlier, are often husband-and-wife teams. There are no restraints that we have found on locating your charter on church property. What is a clear conflict of interest and what is termed a "comingling" of funds in accounting terms happens when the church and state funds mix when the organization is organized as one entity that includes the church and the charter school (or private school). Donations are listed on the 990, a tell in the data that these are from the congregation. One such team of pastors in Yuma, Arizona, took over $392,000 in salaries for a school with a student population of 1,590 students. The school property is owned by the church. There is no evidence (i.e., a separate IRS 990) that the pastors, who are listed as president and vice president of the corporation, are paid anything directly from the church's operations. Several family members of those ministers are also on the payroll. Multiple calls and email requests for documentation that there is a separate organization were ignored, and requests to speak to the listed owners were denied. This is not a lone case. Certainly brothers, priests, and nuns teaching at a Catholic school receive their teaching salaries from that school end of the operations.

In other states, there are charter schools using Horace Mann's name and claiming they are running Christian charter schools that Horace Mann would have deemed appropriate uses of state educational funding. How do these groups justify their mixing of church and school roles?

The argument for these arrangements is that often these pastors are a husband-and-wife team, and the combination saves the school (and the church) money. In some cases this is true.

When the "Saving Money" Quote Actually Happens

Data on this subject gleaned from IRS 990s show this to be the case in the majority of charter schools with populations under 199 students; however, once the number of students climbs to the next ranges of students, another pattern emerges. A comparison of salaries of top management at charters and district superintendents (illustrated in Chapter 5 and repeated in this chapter) shows that there is indeed money to be made as a charter holder.

A disappointing set of rulings by our current Supreme Court seems to fly in the face of the Blaine Amendments[4] language barring the use of public funds for sectarian schools that is in most state constitutions but is being ignored by acting as if the funds are being "given" to the parents to act on their own choices.

Board policies at public schools do not allow board members to benefit financially from their relationship with the school district. That policy is one of the key elements of local, elected oversight of the schools.

Reviews of FY 2020 IRS 990s found multiple paid board members on a significant portion of charter school boards. One such "board member" was being paid as such at five different charter corporations. His wisdom in operating charters is questionable, as he went bankrupt at his own charter, and several others he was affiliated with failed or are failing. In a district this would be called "nepotism." School boards have policies and rules against this practice.

Who decides how much management makes at these private businesses? Superintendent salaries are negotiated by the board, as are benefits for this position. Justifications for large salaries at charters as discussed in their annual audits talk about this subject using the following language: "The board looked at the marketplace when determining compensation for the leaders of the charter." Data from FY 2020 salaries for charter holders illustrate that this is true for what are termed "marketplace" positions for CEOs. That is, they do not compare to superintendent salaries at similar-sized school districts. All of this malaise and profiteering at the expense of teachers and children could have been avoided if the original intent of Ray Budde's charter model was used instead of "market education."

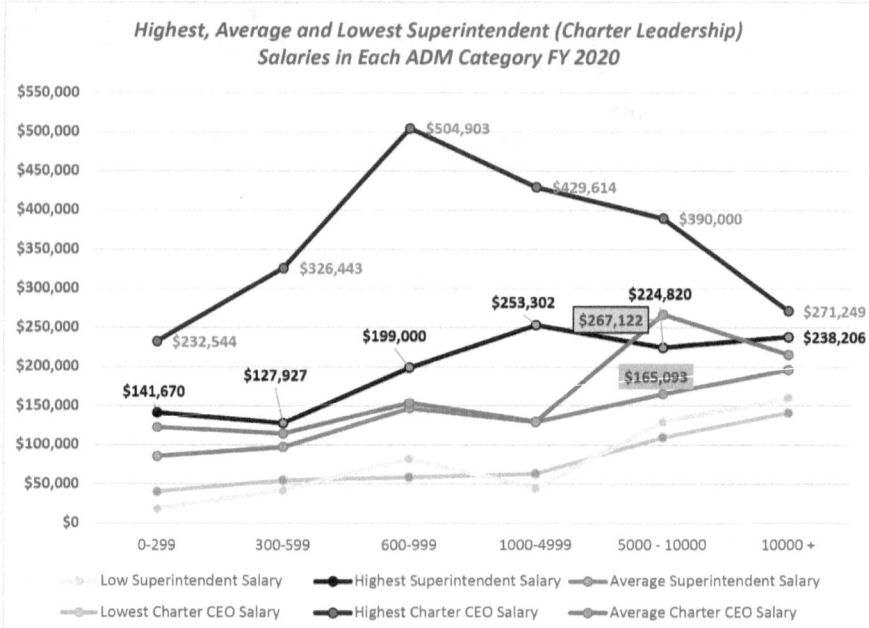

Figure 6.1. Comparison of Top Administrator Salaries at Arizona Charters and Districts by Population Served
Source: Survey of superintendents' salaries by Grand Canyon Institute FY 2020 and IRS 990 data for charter salaries.

The Original Intent of the Originator of the Charter Concept Did Not Include Sectarian Charters

The original charter models prevented the capitalistic greed that we see engaged in at private charters from prevailing. This is still true where charters are under the financial oversight of local school districts (i.e., the funding is distributed to the district and dispensed to the charter from there).

When Dr. Budde of the University of Massachusetts proposed the concept of chartering schools, the charters he described were organized by certified teachers and funded and controlled by the local school board. Teachers would be in charge of these schools and covered under collective bargaining agreements preserving their rights and benefits under those agreements. Dr. Budd's charter idea was taken over and turned into the free market, corporate-driven model that constitutes most of today's charter industry.

The charter model introduced by Dr. Budde would never have included church-owned charter schools funded by taxpayer sources. As a young undergraduate at the University of Massachusetts at Salem, the author had the opportunity to participate in presentations by Dr. Budde regarding his model, a model notably supported by Albert Shanker and the American Federation of Teachers (AFT). This acceptance by the AFT flies in the face of those claiming that the teachers' unions block innovation at district schools. The AFT withdrew support for charters when the new model, privately owned charters, came into being.

Several books and articles by Paul E. Peterson give inaccurate accounts of Dr. Budde's model and his intent. Those writings have a distinct bias toward Christian nationalist notions regarding who should be in charge of our public school funding. Dr. Budde's model[5] is given lip service on some charter lobbying sites advocating for "choice." A link to the ERIC collections with a link to the original model is provided in the endnotes to this chapter. It was the model used by the district-run charters in the author's school district from 1999 to 2005. It successfully created three charters that exist now under the capitalistic model, as the district chose not to continue the programs; two elementary schools in small towns and one high school (small) all left the district as a "conservative" group took over the board and did not support the district having charters.

The next chapter delves into the history of the reasons Horace Mann and the founders did not want sectarian schools funded from public sources.

NOTES

1. https://www.cato.org/blog/education-constitution#:~:text=Where%2C%20in%20the%20Constitution%2C%20is,a%20taxpayer%E2%80%90%E2%80%8Bfunded%20education

2. Ibid.

3. https://azdor.gov/sites/default/files/media/REPORTS_CREDITS_2022_fy2021-private-school-tuition-org-credit-report.pdf

4. https://mtsu.edu/first-amendment/article/1036/blaine-amendments

5. https://eric.ed.gov/?id=ED295298

Chapter 7

Why We Have Separation of Church and State

While nearly all of the founders of our country practiced some form of Christianity, they agreed that the federal government should not require a religious test for holding office in the republic. Article VI of the Constitution clearly states that there should be "no religious test" for holding federal office. A thorough reading of the literature and historic record leads to the conclusion that none of the founders believed in the complete separation of religion and the government. We note that the phrase "separation of church and state" is not found in the Constitution or the Bill of Rights.

In the introduction to this book, we discussed the inclusion of religion as important to the future states that came out of the territories in the Northwest Ordinances (both versions). These documents preceded the Constitution and the Bill of Rights.

So, where did this phase originate?

As noted in a previous chapter, the phrase "separation of church and state" was part of a letter written to the Danbury Baptist Church in Connecticut in 1802, which went on to state that this "wall of separation" was for the protection of religious communities. The author of that letter was Thomas Jefferson.

It is an often-skipped footnote to history that while he was president, Jefferson allowed religious groups to use properties owned by the Treasury and War Departments to hold religious ceremonies. It is not uncommon for our public schools to allow this same type of use of public facilities for congregations without their own meeting accommodations. This is common practice and was part of this author's experience with Arizona's privately held charter schools as well. Public schools need to be places where the community can gather.

Many state legislatures are attempting to pass legislation allowing the use of state revenues to finance vouchers (euphemistically termed "scholarships") for sectarian private schools. Typically these scholarships (which are de facto vouchers) cover only a fraction of the cost of these private school expenses. The term "opportunity scholarships" is used for several reasons.

1. By allowing the parent to make the "choice" to use the "scholarship" at a sectarian school, the promoters of this "parental choice" initiative believe they have a degree of separation from the religious component of the private school.
2. The state only provides a "scholarship" up to the amount that they would typically send to charter schools in their state. This often is only a third of the cost to attend.
3. The legislators believe that this is just an extension of the "opportunity scholarships" they offer to handicapped children, veterans, and other specialized categories used to initiate "scholarships" in their state.

In fact, this "getting the nose of the camel into the tent" was always a long-range plan in the thinking of Milton Friedman, as he proposed the voucher idea in *Free to Choose* (Friedman & Friedman, 1980) and other works on education in a capitalistic marketplace.

"The only social responsibility of a business is to increase its profits" was part of the essay Friedman wrote over 50 years ago, first published in the *New York Times Magazine*. Today's economists have revisited this statement and discredited this theory.[1] They have concluded that "greed is not good," rather than what fictional capitalist Gordon Gecko in the film *Wall Street* asserted: "Greed, for lack of a better word, is good."

This connection between capitalist economic theories and our democratic republic form of government makes the error of connecting our economic system (free market capitalism) with our governmental system (democratic republic) and public policies. We do well to remember that "White Southerners first fought for 'freedom to choose' in the mid-1950s as it became a national goal as a means of defying the U.S. Supreme Court's 1954 *Brown Vs Board of Education* decision which mandated the desegregation of public schools. Their goal was to create pathways for White families to remove their children from classrooms facing integration."[2]

For Friedman, charter schools were a stopgap measure in response to the overwhelming rejection of vouchers by the public. In his literature, he clearly describes this temporary effort to sidestep the voucher issue. In states with charter schools, voters have consistently and vocally rejected the idea of universal vouchers, aka "state-funded scholarships." Ballot initiatives, our First Amendment right to petition the government, are often used to counteract legislative overreach. Efforts by legislatures to change the rules for ballot initiatives have led to court decisions reversing the victories achieved through these initiatives.

Republican legislatures have ignored the voice of the electorate and continued to legislate expanded "scholarship" programs using taxpayer funds as the primary source of funding. This concept is being pushed on the national level by ALEC, an influencer of "conservative" legislatures financed by firms with an agenda that aims to slowly privatize our public schools. This privatization of public education to include sectarian schools was never the intent of the founders.

In Chapter 4 of this book, we noted that Horace Mann laid out six main principles regarding the republic's interest in funding, governing, and controlling a common public education sustained by an interested public.

1. The public should no longer remain ignorant.
2. That such education should be paid for, controlled, and sustained by an interested public.
3. That this education will be best provided in schools that embrace children from a variety of backgrounds.
4. That this education must be nonsectarian.
5. That this education must be taught by the spirit, methods, and discipline of a free society.
6. That education should be provided by well-trained, professional teachers.

The argument for this separation of public funding from private sectarian schools is deep and was extensively debated in Massachusetts when they established public education in the state. The classic study of this topic is from a Yale student's work in 1929 (Culver, 1929) and in the archives of the Massachusetts Board of Education's collections on Horace Mann's writings. An extensive search of the literature also informs this discussion and includes Mann's notes and writings (Mann et al., 1989) and those of his wife, Mary Peabody, as told in the book *Until Victory* (Tharp, 1953), along with other biographies and critiques of Horace Mann (Taylor, 2010).

Many of the sites traducing Horace Mann's legacy are related to the pro-choice side of the argument about what constitutes a free and appropriate public education.

CONTEXT

When the town of Franklin, Massachusetts, incorporated in 1778, Horace Mann was not yet born. Events were occurring that would shape Horace's worldview, starting with the town's founding.

It is telling that when choosing the name for their new town, the town fathers chose to call in Franklin. The story of this town honoring Benjamin

Franklin in their name is significant because of Franklin's response to this honor and his gift to the town.

The Franklin town fathers, who were religious people, asked Dr. Franklin to purchase a bell for the town's church to mark naming the town Franklin. Franklin demurred and instead offered to purchase and provide a library collection to the town that they had to agree to share with the surrounding communities and their residents. This collection still exists.[3]

Franklin had a limited public school offering when Horace Mann was born on May 4, 1796, into our newly created democratic republic (July 21, 1788). He is said to have read every book in the Franklin collection before he set out for Brown University to be trained as a lawyer. He graduated as head of his class and married Charlotte Messer, the daughter of the dean of the university. This personal history is significant because he was given a limited childhood public education by inadequately trained instructors.

Franklin's gift to Franklin, Massachusetts, like his bequests to Boston and Philadelphia where he dictated the terms of their use, had planted a seed for public education. This seed grew into fruition when Horace Mann came of age.

Franklin's bequests have a legacy of promoting the public's well-being and are some of the wisest choices in the history of philanthropic giving. An article in the online journal *Mental Floss* celebrates Franklin's intent for the use of his bequests and how they benefited the municipalities of Boston and Philadelphia. His gifts of 1,000 pounds sterling to each city became millions because Franklin dictated that the fund be used in an intentional manner.[4]

The article explains Franklin's intent: "The money, he wrote, was to be handled in a very particular way. For the first 100 years, each of the 1,000 pounds sterling would accrue interest and be used to fund loans for young tradesmen starting out in business. Franklin, who had become a printer as the result of a loan given to him, valued resources for apprentices." He also suggested that the proceeds be used for trade schools.

What is clear in all of Franklin's charitable giving is that he preferred to give funds to further educational rather than religious organizations. He was not alone among the founding fathers in this parsing of his fortune.

Chaotic Times for Churches in the Early 1800s

In Massachusetts, where the original goals for a public education were debated and enacted into law, and indeed in the rest of the country at the time, religious practices were in a period of transition. Freedom of religion has always been a primary goal of our republic, as well as freedom from religion if that was your choice. This struggle has recently been detailed in John M. Barry's (2012) *Roger Williams and the Creation of the American Soul*.

Statistics meticulously gathered by Raymond B. Culver (1929) for his doctoral work and book *Horace Mann and Religion in the Massachusetts Public Schools*, describing this conversion of churches from one denomination to another during the early 1800s and the laws enacted in Massachusetts regarding these transfers, show this upheaval in religious beliefs and the turmoil that early promoters of public schooling were trying to avoid in their public schools.

In 1800 there was one Catholic diocese in the northeast, the Diocese of Boston. In 1808 this included Rhode Island, Connecticut, New Hampshire, Vermont, and the current state of Maine. A total of three Catholic churches existed in 1808 (O'Gorman, 1895).

Dr. Joseph Clark, a chronicler of Massachusetts ecclesiastical history, detailed the condition of various sects from 1620 to 1858 (Clark & Congregational Board of Publication, 1858; Clark et al., 1859). The statistics of the time tell a story of religious upheaval.

CHURCH SECTS IN MASSACHUSETTS IN 1800

344 Congregationalist churches
93 Baptist churches
20 Methodist churches
14 Episcopalian churches

8 Quaker meeting places
2 Presbyterian churches (Calvinist)
4 Universalist churches
1 Roman Catholic church

In 1858, after growth in the population and the constitution of various sects, Clark reported:

490 Orthodox Congregationalists
277 Episcopal Methodist congregations
266 Baptist congregations
170 Unitarian churches
135 Universalist congregations
85 Episcopalian congregations
64 Roman Catholic churches
37 Christian churches
24 Friends meetinghouses

21 Free-Will Baptist churches
20 Protestant or independent Methodist churches

15 Second Adventist churches
13 Wesleyan Methodist churches
11 Swedenborgian churches
7 Presbyterian churches
4 Shaker meeting halls
12 unclassified churches

As noted earlier, many of our founding fathers identified as "Deists" or "Unitarians"; still others in the southern and middle states identified as Methodists, Presbyterians, or Baptists. By far the Deists and Unitarians were the norm. To say that the founders had no religious affiliation or belief system is a misrepresentation of their worldview. However, the strife between religious groups informed their writings and their passion to keep religious controversies out of the public sphere.

Nathanael Emmons

Any discussion of influences on Horace Mann's desire to keep sectarianism out of the public schools would be remiss if it failed to discuss the negative experiences that Mann endured in his family's church, where Nathanael Emmons presided as minister.

Emmons was one of the originators of the "New Light" or "New Divinity" school originating with Jonathan Edwards and developed by Samuel Hopkins. Calvinists who adhered to this kind of thinking are often referred to as "Strict Calvinists" or "Consistent Calvinists." As a high school student at Central Catholic in Allentown, Pennsylvania, one of our readings was Edward's sermon "Sinners in the Hands of an Angry God."[5]

Horace Mann and his dear mother were traumatized when his brother, Stephen Mann (born in 1792), drowned in Uncas Pond. Stephen had gone swimming on a Sunday, skipping Emmons's service. From the pulpit, Emmons condemned Stephen Mann to hell, which caused his mother to visibly pale as she sat next to Horace at the Sunday service. Mann decided he could no longer participate in a religious system that was based on a vindictive deity. He became a Unitarian and remained so until his death at Antioch College in Yellow Springs, Ohio, on August 2, 1859, of typhoid fever. (Note: Although he had remarried to Mary Peabody, one of the historically famous Peabody sisters, Horace Mann chose to be buried next to his first wife, Charlotte Messer Mann.)

The turmoil and animosity among the religious sects of the time and the events of the "Evangelical Awakening," also known as the "Orthodox Reaction," were major factors in the Massachusetts Board of Education's desire to keep sectarianism out of the public schools.

NOTES

1. https://www.forbes.com/advisor/investing/milton-friedman-social-responsibility-of-business

2. https://www.washingtonpost.com/outlook/2021/09/27/school-choice-developed-way-protect-segregation-abolish-public-schools

3. https://02038.com/2009/02/exterior-franklin-public-library

4. https://www.mentalfloss.com/article/627475/200-year-old-gift-from-benjamin-franklin-to-boston-and-philadelphia
5. https://www.blueletterbible.org/Comm/edwards_jonathan/Sermons/Sinners.cfm

REFERENCES

Barry, J. M. (2012). *Roger Williams and the creation of the American soul: Church, state, and the birth of liberty*. New York: Viking.

Clark, J. S., & Congregational Board of Publication. (1858). *A historical sketch of the Congregational churches in Massachusetts, from 1620 to 1858*. Boston: Congregational Board of Publication.

Clark, J. S., Dexter, H. M., Quint, A. H., Langworthy, I. P., Cushing, C., & Burnham, S. (1859). *The Congregational Quarterly*. Boston, New York.

Culver, R. B. (1929). *Horace Mann and religion in the Massachusetts public schools*. New Haven, CT: Yale University Press.

Friedman, M., & Friedman, R. D. (1980). *Free to choose: A personal statement* (1st ed.). New York: Harcourt Brace Jovanovich.

Mann, H., Dwight, E. A., Mann, M. T. P., Peabody, E. P., & Massachusetts Historical Society. (1989). *The papers of Horace Mann*. Boston: Massachusetts Historical Society.

O'Gorman, T. (1895). *A history of the Roman Catholic Church in the United States*. New York: Christian Literature Co.

Taylor, B. P. (2010). *Horace Mann's troubling legacy: The education of democratic citizens*. Lawrence: University Press of Kansas.

Tharp, L. H. (1953). *Until victory: Horace Mann and Mary Peabody* (1st ed.). Boston: Little, Brown.

Chapter 8

"That Education Should Be Provided by Well-Trained, Professional Teachers"

In the previous chapters, we noted that Horace Mann sought to create a common school system that would be rigorous enough to compete with the best private schools, thereby enhancing the opportunity of the individuals paying for those educational options to choose their local public schools. The ultimate goal was not to make private schools or sectarian schools obsolete but to create schools for the republic where all classes and belief systems would find a publicly financed option. Public education was meant to mix all classes together in the common enterprise of living and participating in a republic. In order for this to occur, the republic needed to provide educational opportunities for those seeking to enter the teaching profession to become well versed in the liberal arts and astute at understanding teaching methodologies.

The proposals now afloat in several states using universal vouchers include provisions for payment for homeschooling and micro-schools. Neither of these requires a well-trained professional teacher. It is ironic that people who feel they are capable of homeschooling likely got their own education at a school, either private or public. In New Hampshire, the push is on to get people on the lowest end of the socioeconomic scale to move into homeschooling and micro-schools.

At the time that Horace Mann initiated normal schools, there were limited colleges and universities in the United States. The population was mostly uneducated except in states that had already established public schools, such as New York and Massachusetts.

Teaching is a performing art. It is a profession that requires knowledge of and mastery of many subject areas. Teachers need to know what to teach and how to present that core knowledge to their students. The American Teachers Association (ATA), which is today the National Education Association (NEA), has a key role to play in ensuring that our students are prepared to live in a republic. This includes incorporating many of the hard-won changes in the makeup of our society. The National Education Association receives a great deal of criticism for its positions on social change. This continues a proud tradition of the organization representing most of our professional teachers.

That organization went through many transformations during its history, as described below:

- 1865: At the summer convention, ATA president J. P. Wilkersham denounces slavery, and the ATA recommends that no seceded states be readmitted to the Union until they agree to provide a free public school system for black as well as white children, one of the promises to the Civil War black volunteers that joined the Union army.
- 1866: The ATA opens membership to women, followed in 1869 by the hiring of the first woman president of the ATA, Emily Rice.
- 1869: The ATA combines with other smaller teacher associations to become the NEA.
- 1892: The Committee of Ten: "After the Civil War, publicly funded high schools began to appear alongside the privately funded academies that prepared students for college. By the 1890s various, often competing academic philosophies—rote memorization vs. critical thinking, working trades vs. college bound—could be found in secondary education curricula throughout America. In 1892, NEA charged a ten-member Committee on Secondary School Studies with 'taking stock of current practice in America's high schools and making recommendations for future practice.' The Committee of Ten's 1894 Report made recommendations that established curriculum standards for a generation and continue to have both positive (movement away from classic Greek curricula, expanded scope of who is educated) and negative (standardization framework rooted in White colonialism) impacts on how American students receive their educations."[1] In this history, contemporary historians added the comments regarding the standardized framework rooted in white colonialism.
  - When a charter or private school touts their "back to basics" approach, this is one of the items they push back on, assuming that all teachers are now framing their teaching of history through this lens.
- 1920: Public education becomes a national priority, and mandatory schooling is established for the elementary grades. The NEA moves to its modern structure of affiliated state and local unions with delegates sent to a national Representative Assembly. This aligns the organization to a structure that is consistent with a representative democracy.

- 1928: The Southern Association of Schools and Colleges refuses to accredit schools for African American students. The NEA and ATA react by creating the Joint Committee for Justice. These moves further alienate the organization from the "conservative" right.
- 1940s: As a statement on principles, the NEA responds to its own affiliates' discrimination by refusing to hold its Representative Assemblies in cities that discriminate.
- 1954: The targeting of black educators by those attempting to sidestep *Brown v. Board of Education* leads to the establishment of a $1 million fund designed to "protect and promote the professional, civil, and human rights of educators," and the NEA works with the ATA to support those teachers. The birth of what many complain about as union activism to protect educators from unjust firings leads to anti–teacher union sentiment.
- 1967: The NEA, now merged with the ATA, elects a Hispanic educator as its leader. Their political work and lobbying result in the passage of the Bilingual Education Act in 1968. This becomes the target of groups insisting on English immersion who then work to eliminate, at the state level, bilingual education. The fight continues to this day, notably in Arizona and Florida.
- 1968: The NEA elects its first black educator as president. The organization establishes a Center for Human Relations, currently known as Human and Civil Rights. This move again creates tensions between segregationists and the "moral majority" and the teachers' association.
- 1970s: The NEA creates the Ethnic and Minority Affairs Committee, ensuring minority representation on NEA governing boards.
- 1974: The NEA leads the effort to eliminate mandatory maternity leaves for pregnant teachers.
- 1980s: The NEA admits all educational staff members, including support workers, to join the union and become a part of collective bargaining.
- 2015: The NEA commits to the eradication of institutional racism, a move that is again seen as "woke education" by the far-right groups pushing for "school choice" and vouchers.
- 2018: The Representative Assembly adopts NEA Resolution I-52, which acknowledges the existence of white supremacy culture as a primary root cause of institutional racism, structural racism, and white privilege.

The teachers' "unions" have always been a target for missives directed at public education. In fact, as a rule of thumb, the NEA has kept pace with various amendments to the Constitution and our treatment of minorities, ethnic groups, and differing sexual orientations. Their critique of "a white supremacy culture" has a long and proud history. They have also pushed back on efforts to use public funding to allow the public to "choose" to go to sectarian and segregated schools.

Is it any wonder that Turning Point USA raises funding and membership by defining public education as the enemy in its "War on American Culture"? This effort is directed at students and directed against public education. The organization's mission is to identify, educate, train, and organize students to promote the principles of freedom, free markets, and limited government. Turning Point USA believes that every young person can be enlightened to what they term true free market values.

Here is one of those values, as touted by Milton Friedman in *Freedom to Choose*: "The only moral imperative of a business is to make money for its stockholders." Capitalism, Mr. Kirk and Turning Point USA, is our economic system, not our system of government, which is a democratic republic. They are not one and the same.

No one has ever suggested that parents should not be able to choose where their students go to school. My grandchildren go to a Catholic School, as did I as a youth. Their parents and I paid for that religious choice. Teachers in charters accept lower pay and less benefits than those in our public schools. This author started charters in New Hampshire and continues to support well-regulated charters. These choices are financially a free choice.

The real goal of "choice" is taking "backpacks full of cash" from our public school systems and placing that money into privately owned buildings and educational programs.

This effort is also an assault on the teaching profession as represented by the NEA. One of the first moves in states seeking to use charters and vouchers is to become "right to work" states, where union membership cannot be a condition of employment. The correct term for this is "union busting."

Teachers in charters and private schools struggle to meet their basic needs in environments where there are limited benefits, poor retirement plans, and low wages. Turnover in these schools is high, especially among lay employees.

If we truly care about the quality of life for our professional educators, we need to ask pointed questions about our choices, now funded by taxpayer funds:

- What are the pay scales for your teachers?
- What do you provide for health insurance and other benefits?
- How are you providing for your employees' retirement years?
- What is the participation rate of in your 401(k) plans?

Unionization is rare in charter schools and nonexistent in private schools.

DE-PROFESSIONALIZING THE TEACHING PROFESSION

We are using "choice" to turn teaching into a nonprofessional occupation. We would be wise to recall that until the early 1920s, medicine was a career rather than a profession. The work of the Flexner Commission (run by Abraham Flexner, a private school operator and teacher) created the standards and professionalism that is present in today's medical professions. Certification as a doctor did not require internships or extended study prior to the Flexner Report.

When we started turning medicine back into a "business," the result was health maintenance organizations (HMOs). Doctors were no longer deciding what treatment they would be able to provide.

Private schools are just that, private. So are their financial books and how they are spending that taxpayer-funded voucher cash. Data gathered for and contained within this book show that management in these "free market" enterprises is siphoning off funds intended for the education of our children into financial boons for ownership. Benefits for management often include a package far superior to those offered for teachers.

At the same time, these mega-charters and church-run enterprises are using capitalist thinking to push out locally owned and operated charters that have high academic performances and district schools with A-plus ratings. Fratricide is a fact in the charter and voucher marketplace. Statistics from FY 2022 in Arizona, a "choice" state, validate this fratricide assertion. The goal is to eventually usurp and take over our public schools and acquire their properties, which are largely paid for in full. Only large-scale charter groups and private schools with the backing of their churches have the capacity for this type of hostile takeover.

The public in a republic has no vested interest in sponsoring privately owned choices. The republic has no vested interest in untrained teachers running private schools or in your choice to homeschool your child, which is often done via a micro-school.

The entitlement mentality created by the charter and voucher industries to claim public money for those private choices has little to do with educational needs and much to do with the effort to remove the public from our educational policies. The rise of charter schools, with limited safeguards regarding the training of their teachers, and vouchers with no requirements for the training of their teachers, is a direct slap at Horace Mann's intent.

Table 8.1. Market Consolidation in the Arizona Charter "Free Market" in FY 2022

Charter Sites	Actual Charters	Charter Corporations
608	417	234

Top 10 Charter Corporations

ADM Top 10	Sites	Charters	Corporations
102,611	167	138	10

% of ADM	% of Sites	% of Charters	% of Corporations
46.47	27.47	33.09	4.27

Top 20 Charter Corporations

ADM Top 20	Sites	Charters	Corporations
134,364	216	157	20

% of ADM	% of Sites	% of Charters	% of Corporations
60.85	35.53	37.65	8.55

All Other Charters

All Other ADM	Sites	Charters	Corporations
86,451	392	260	214

% of ADM	% of Sites	% of Charters	% of Corporations
39.15	64.47	62.35	91.45

Source: Arizona Department of Education data on ADM, FY 2022, collated by Grand Canyon Institute.

Table 8.2. Market Consolidation in the Arizona Charter "Free Market," Illustrating the Effect of Consolidation and the Federal Influx of Aid through ESSER Funding in FY 2022

Charter Sites Lost FY 2018–FY 2023	Charters Sites Lost Since 2014
50	101
13.16%	26.58%
	Federal Dollars Subsidizing Charters, FY 2022
Total Charter Corporations That Ended FY 2022 in the Red Despite PPP Loans and ESSER Funding	Collected by Charters From ESSER Funds
89	$252,954,592.25

Total PPP Taken by Charters From Other Federal Government Programs	$52,127,700.00
Average PPP Amount Taken by Charters per ADM	$788.27

Source: Arizona Department of Education data on ADM, FY 2022, collated by Grand Canyon Institute.

"THAT EDUCATION SHOULD BE PROVIDED BY WELL-TRAINED, PROFESSIONAL TEACHERS"

Ronald Reagan is often cited by those wishing to privatize our public schools, as someone who would stand up for a parent's right to choose. He and the Republican Party sought to establish federal tax credits, not deductions, for this purpose—an idea that makes sense and eliminates the need for vouchers for this purpose.

- He also spoke to the issue of where religious training belonged, "in the home," although he also spoke about allowing students to hold organized prayer at school.
- Reagan was a firm believer in local control of education finances and governance.
- He was also a clear defender of teachers as worthy stewards of our public schools. When it came time for a private citizen to be a part of the space shuttle crew, he famously stated, "It should be one of America's finest, a teacher."
  - Being from New Hampshire and knowing Christa McAuliffe, this Republican at the time supported Reagan's platform, including that there should be a right to work, where unions could not force members to join as a condition of employment.
- The party's system of block grants to the states put the power over these funds back in the state and local arenas.[2]

President Reagan also knew that teachers could be trusted to instill American values into their students. It is a little-known fact that a great many of our teachers in his time and now are former soldiers, airmen, and sailors who actively served their country in the armed services and are now serving again as teachers, principals, and superintendents in their communities. Donald Trump accidently acknowledged this fact when he spoke about arming teachers in New Hampshire as a way to prevent gun deaths at schools. He said that a lot of our great teachers could be armed and spoke about the fact that many of those teachers have military training.

Tax Credits That Are Covered by IRS Rules

The federal credit for education that is on the books is the American Opportunity Tax Credit.

> The AOTC helps defray the cost of higher education expenses for tuition, certain fees and course materials for four years. It is a tax credit of up to $2,500 of

the cost of tuition, certain required fees and course materials needed for attendance and paid during the tax year. Also, 40 percent of the credit for which you qualify that is more than the tax you owe (up to $1,000) can be refunded to you.[3]

The credits can't be used for a higher education at an uncertified institution.

That education should be provided by well-trained, professional teachers continues to be under attack when we allow private schools and micro-schools to hire untrained, high school–educated staff.

NOTES

1. Sabrina Holcomb, 2021, "The History of the NEA," https://www.nea.org/about-nea/mission-vision-values/history-nea

2. *Republican Party Platform of 1980*, American Presidency Project, https://www.presidency.ucsb.edu/documents/republican-party-platform-1980

3. https://www.irs.gov/credits-deductions/individuals/education-credits-questions-and-answers

Chapter 9

Restoring Hope to Our Educational Efforts in a Republic

Horace Mann and the founders had high ideals and high hopes for public education in our republic. Illiteracy and a lack of mathematical and science instruction, as we have shown, were hindering the progress of the new country. Benjamin Franklin knew this when he said, "A republic, if you can keep it," as a reply to what form of government we would establish in our country.

The need for a public that understood and cherished the idea of a morally driven democratic republic and the importance of keeping religious bias out of our government was critical to the success of that republic. We were not founded as a "Christian nation." We were founded as a republic.

Many of the current and past critics of our public schools cite the loss of organized school prayer and facing up to the good and the bad of our history as creating godless students who grow up to hate our country. As Thomas Jefferson and Horace Mann knew, the exact opposite is true.

Public education is meant to preserve our republic and cherish its ideals. Teaching about times when those stated ideals were not being met is a part of that story. As a teacher, I often reminded my students that the greatest generation of Americans and their country won the Second World War by reconquering territory that the fascists had taken over. The big difference was that our country returned the lands and property of those lands to the original owners. Teaching about our faults without balancing that teaching with the overwhelming evidence that we have grown as a nation and work toward a more perfect union is foolhardy. As an administrator, I made sure that did not happen in the public and charter schools I oversaw.

Consider this question: Has the move to privatize education and pay for those private educations brought us closer together or pushed us further apart?

Recruiting for our armed forces is down. Politically we are further apart than at any time since the Civil War.

At the local level, we have forgotten who the "home team" is. It is and always will be the local public school's team. Friday night lights and other cherished parts of our community life are fading with the re-sorting of ourselves and our children into different types of choices for our schooling.

This type of sorting was always available. That was your "freedom to choose." What it never included was payment for the choice of going to a privately owned and operated "publicly funded" school.

As far as our monetary commitments to education, we need to be, as the Beach Boys said, "true to your school." The only schools that truly belong to the people and are governed by the people are the communities' public schools.

There has always been tension between our republic's economic model, capitalism, and our political model, a democratic republic. The tension comes from how both of these ideas work *in tandem* in a republic. In his best-selling book *Tailspin: The People and Forces Behind America's Fifty-Year Fall—And Those Fighting to Reverse It*, Steven Brill articulates the reason for this tension:

> There has always been an inherent tension in societies that are politically democratic and economically capitalist. The former is based on equality; the latter is fueled by the participant's dreams of accruing more wealth than the other guy. Maintaining political equality in a land of wealth inequality requires a delicate balance.
>
> If the forces of political equality prevail so totally that they do too much to equalize wealth, such as with confiscatory taxes, the incentives and energy of a capitalist system are eroded. If wealth inequality gets too extreme, the power of the wealthy can be deployed to erode democracy. (Brill, 2018)

AN ECONOMIC VERSUS A POLITICAL THEORY OF ACTION

The charter and voucher movements are founded on an economic theory of action applied to publicly funded education in a democratic republic. Politically this meant that decision making about public education shifted from the local level to the state and federal levels. The model has also become politicized, with multiple political parties, Democratic, Republican, and Libertarian, participating in the legislative actions authorizing public funds to contracted educational service providers.

The Libertarian Party, which has since backed away from Friedman's use of government funding to finance education in a democratic republic, wrote their seminal educational platform regarding public education in 1980. The vice-presidential candidate in that critical year was none other than David Koch of the billionaire Koch brothers.

The euphemistic descriptions of charter schools promulgated by the National Conference of State Legislatures were designed to "ease" the public's perception about the real goals of the economic theory behind "school choice": a purely capitalistic marketplace for educational services. Those goals were articulated in the 1980 Libertarian Party platform, which states the real educational goals of this movement regarding the education of children in a republic.

Is Friedman's ultimate goal regarding education really what we want to be headed toward? In 2004 he restated that ultimate goal: "In my ideal world, government would not be responsible for providing education any more than it is for providing food and clothing." Four months before his death in 2006, when he spoke to a meeting of the conservative American Legislative Exchange Council (ALEC), he was especially frank. Addressing how to give parents control of their children's education, Friedman said, "The ideal way would be to abolish the public school system and eliminate all the taxes that pay for it." That would include all the funding that supports your charters, homeschooling, micro-schools, and private choices.

In Arizona, one of the first "tax credit" program ideas was to offload the provision of charitable food and clothing to charities, including sectarian organizations. As a lazy Catholic and knowing a great deal when I saw it, I continue to donate to St. Vincent de Paul for up to $800 in tax credit on my Arizona taxes. The state has made donations to charter, private nonprofit, and district schools eligible for these credits. New Hampshire, which is mimicking Arizona, initiated an Education Tax Credit Program in FY (for business profit taxes, business enterprise taxes, and interest and dividend taxes). The amounts take a serious toll on New Hampshire's state tax collections, as does the recent uptick to $9,000 for charter school grants, which had a similar boost to the amount going to public schools but tempered by the equalization formulas in the state.[1]

The fact that this law exists allowed the New Hampshire Supreme Court to vacate *Duncan v. The State of New Hampshire*,[2] which was filed as a case against using school tuition tax-credit revenues to fund a sectarian education. New Hampshire does not have an income or a sales tax. It collects taxes on liquor using its state-controlled stores (which offer discounted prices to non-residents purchasing liquor at the conveniently located border stores), lotteries, and the rooms and meals tax.

Logical Conclusion

The logical conclusion of enacting these policies is that individuals would be able to choose *whatever they could afford to pay for educational services in a future republic that defines itself as a capitalist state.* Economic decisions regarding what you can afford at the individual level would drive your consumer choices—a true capitalist model, driven by individual choice and that individual's ability to pay. We have evidence regarding how that model would work in the historical record of our republic. We have been there before.

Historical Context

The 1980 Libertarian educational platform described educational choice *as it existed in the United States in 1919, prior to universal, taxpayer-funded public education.* The educational results of that model were the highest illiteracy rates among the general population in our republic's history, widespread poverty, and a low standard of living. There was a reason that the first national political moves into education at the elementary and high school levels were termed national defense initiatives. Illiteracy plagued the nation's armed forces in the First and Second World Wars. Education and the taxes used to support it were purposefully designed to promote the general welfare, *not individual economic choices.*

The words prior to "general welfare" in the Constitution are related to our common defense, another area where the country has debated over who is responsible for paying the bills for our nation's military expenditures. There was a reason that a standing army and navy were not established immediately after the nation was founded. State and local militias are one of the reasons the Constitution's Second Amendment was written. It doesn't read, "A well-regulated" national army. It says, "A well-regulated militia." Article I, section 8, of the U.S. Constitution grants Congress the power to "lay and collect Taxes, Duties, Imposts, and Excises, to pay the Debts and provide for the common defense and general Welfare of the United States."

The Backpacks Full of Cash Lie

Citizens of this country have always had the freedom to choose where they sent their children for an education. The Libertarian education platform is describing the same "freedom to choose" that was available to all parents (again financially driven) to choose which type of school they sent their children to prior to 1994. In addition to this "choice," they also, after 1919, had a publicly financed choice of where to send their child to school. That publicly financed choice is the only one the states, localities, and the people agreed to be financially responsible for. Children in a republic are not backpacks full of cash.

The difference after 1994 is that in some states, charter and voucher laws have allowed parents the freedom to claim a government subsidy to finance their individual choice. That subsidy is paid out to private contractors from tax revenues. Isn't this what conservatives usually call an "entitlement mentality" (i.e., I am entitled to an educational choice that the general public pays for with their taxes)?

The "government schools" system derided in this platform came into play after mandatory schooling laws were enacted in all states in 1919. *Within a year, child labor laws were also enacted, encouraged by the burgeoning labor movement at that time.* The two laws are connected.

Personal Financial Responsibility Is a Capitalistic and American Value

When choice advocates utter the words "freedom to choose," they are describing a freedom that individual citizens *already had.* There is nothing in the mandatory requirements to educate children in the republic that prevents a private citizen from choosing another form of education, as long as they paid for it—true capitalism. The republic's interest is in making a public common school system available so that the type of education that benefits the ideals of a republican form of government is provided—engaged, literate citizens able to participate in a capitalistic economic model.

This freedom to choose also includes homeschooling, which is also a choice. States legislated homeschooling into mandatory education laws during the 20th century, legalizing this choice but not funding it. Funding homeschool parents for choosing to educate their child in isolation from the community is a misappropriation of taxpayer funds, a handout to those choosing to homeschool. What is unclear about that title? Homeschool. I am choosing to educate my child at home my way.

Those taxpayer-sourced funds are being used to support an unregistered, unsupervised education provided by the parents. The new rules make access to those funds an entitlement. Equally shocking is the way those funds are doled out. States use a system that is akin to the use of welfare debit cards. This use of debit cards is decried by conservatives but perfectly acceptable to the "choice" industry. Is it any surprise that the documented abuse rate is 15% in both cases?

This, then, is Friedman's Folly, describing a "freedom to choose" and then attaching a monetary entitlement to funding of that choice from state and federal taxes. That is socialistic, not capitalistic, thinking carried to an extreme.

The legislature in Arizona cites the state constitution as giving them the authority to pay for private schooling choices, homeschooling, and charter schools. While the establishment of "public charter schools" fits the constitution's current definition of the educational requirements of the state, it does not, no matter how it is couched (e.g., well, it is the parent who is choosing; therefore it isn't the state funding the private school; it is the parent's choice). We have shown that common schools had a specific meaning: schools held in common by the public.

> The legislature shall enact such laws as shall provide for the establishment and maintenance of a general and uniform public school system, which system shall include:
>
> 1. Kindergarten schools.
> 2. Common schools.
> 3. High schools.
> 4. Normal schools.
> 5. Industrial schools.
> 6. Universities, which shall include an agricultural college, a school of mines, and such other technical schools as may be essential, until such time as it may be deemed advisable to establish separate state institutions of such character.

The promoters of tax funding for school choice need to make logical sense.

We do not expect the government to finance our choice to own a gun. It's a choice we make and a choice we are responsible for. Defenders of the Second Amendment want to be able to choose and to limit restrictions on gun ownership.

The NRA's support of school choice advocacy groups such as Turning Point USA is not defending freedom to choose; it is defending the government subsidizing my choice (i.e., an education that the government has enabled for me by subsidizing its cost). Federal and state money is involved in this transfer of responsibility for payment.

An old argument for the funding of choice models used to be, "Well, we subcontract for highway construction and the delivery of a usable highway with construction companies. This is the same thing." No, we own those roads when the contractor is finished, and we control the construction process with regulations and oversight. Roads not built to specification have to be redone at the contractor's expense.

Our public schools are not perfect. They are, however, the only locally controlled and governed schools in the current mix. In our small towns and in sections of each city, they are the hearts of the local community. They are the only educational choice where the public has a say in how they are operated at the local level. They are open for the public to hold meetings and to use as emergency spaces in times of natural or man-made disasters. They are the only educational choice that the public owns.

The rules for taking a subsidy for your choice need to be changed or we are going to bankrupt our state budgets. In the fall of 2019, the U.S. Department of Education counted 4.7 million American children in private schools (sectarian and nonsectarian). At an average of $8,500 per entitlement, the figure for the country comes to $40 billion. These are new to the budget costs for students. In that same year, the United States spent $752 billion (federal, state, and local spending) on 50.8 million students in public and charter schools. This equates to spending of around $15,000 per student, the majority of which comes from local sources. States are creating a new draw with their contributions to private educations and claiming they are saving money by stating that they spend less per student as a state (90% of a full ADM cost) on voucher students. To counter this argument, the pro-choice superintendent of public education cites work from the Goldwater Institute that is not only biased, as the author is a direct beneficiary of the choice marketplace, but is claimed to be unbiased by Superintendent Horne. Really.

The cases cited by the Supreme Court's recent rulings allowing (forcing) states to pay for a sectarian choice based on the plaintiff's claim of religious freedom fly in the face of a different Supreme Court's logic in 2004 when it ruled in *Locke v. Davey*. A student who opted to attend a divinity school program was denied access to Washington State's publicly funded scholarship program for colleges.

In *Locke v. Davey*, 540 U.S. 712 (2004), the Supreme Court ruled that a generous college scholarship program in Washington State that did not allow a student to use his publicly funded scholarship to major in theology did not violate his First Amendment rights of free exercise of religion or free speech. It was not until the current Supreme Court's majority changed that this type of ruling would shift toward "freedom of religion" issues. Look for the current Court to upend *Locke v. Davey* in the future. The current Supreme Court is for religious choices while it overturns precedent in cases where other choices are at stake.

What is really happening is that the shift in our interpretation of what type of education is eligible for public funding is going to give those invested in "choice" a chance to capture more of the dollars we spend on educating our children.

Vouchers and STO scholarships are overwhelmingly going to high-income zip codes and sectarian choices. These are costs that we were not bearing prior to this giveaway of our tax revenues. They represent taxation without representation as control of these tax dollars moves from the state to the private company's discretion.

At the same time, we are moving toward a system of schools that allows us to organize the schools by race, religion, and ethnicity. This is not the way to ensure liberty and justice for all in a republic.

Horace Mann pointed the way to do that in a republic. This education must be provided by well-trained, professional teachers. Horace Mann believed in the power of public education to achieve social unity and individual freedom. In conclusion, Horace's main principles for public common schools are as relevant today as they were when he first articulated them.

His six main principles for public schools were the following:

1. The public should no longer remain ignorant.
2. Such education should be paid for, controlled, and sustained by an interested public.
3. This education will be best provided in schools that embrace children from a variety of backgrounds.
4. This education must be nonsectarian.
5. This education must be taught by the spirit, methods, and discipline of a free society.
6. This education must be provided by well-trained, professional teachers.

Those declaring their private and charter schools as "back to basics" and parents seeking schools that fulfill the promise of the Civil War–era recruiting poster on the front of this book should look no further than our public common schools.

If those schools are not what you deem are the best for your child, your faith, or your political outlook at the time, then you are free to choose.

With great freedom comes the accompanying great responsibility—moral and financial responsibility.

We expect this in our dealings in a capitalist economy. We choose our service providers based on our free choice and ability to pay for that choice. That is what true capitalism is about, not some economist's interpretation that leads to an entitlement mentality that draws funds from the state and federal governments.

Be true to YOUR schools. Friday night lights for the home team live at those schools, not at a privately owned educational enterprise with no real connection to its community.

The schools that you own, public common schools, the schools meant for all of us.

NOTES

1. htttps://www.revenue.nh.gov/assistance/education-tax-credit.htm
2. htttps://www.revenue.nh.gov/laws/documents/140828-duncan.pdf

Chapter 10

"That This Education Will Be Best Provided in Schools That Embrace Children From a Variety of Backgrounds"

We are rapidly becoming a nation where we segregate ourselves into groups defined by economic ranking, religious belief, and ethnicity.

A macro-analysis of where children are going to schools of choice tends to show that this is not the case. But micro-analysis of the same data tells a different story.

Scottsdale, Arizona, has a school district with a large population of students who choose to attend Scottsdale instead of their home districts. The ethnicity of its school population shows this diversity (see Figures 10.1 and 10.2).

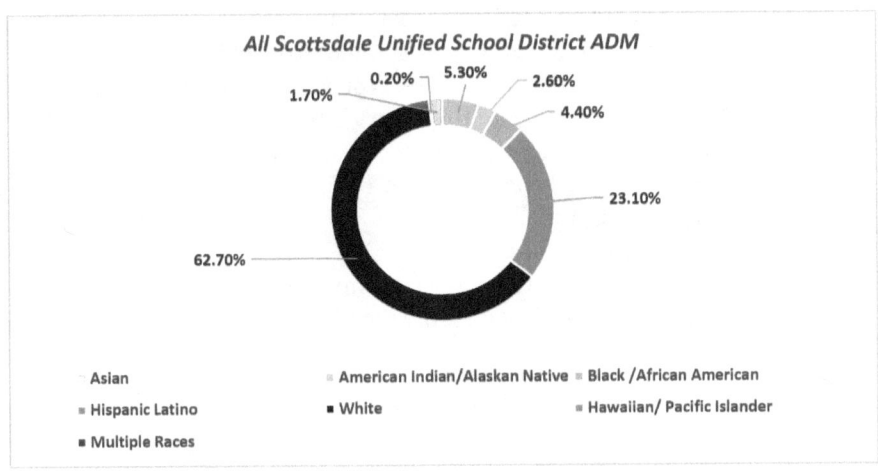

Figure 10.1. Ethnicity of Students in Scottsdale Unified School District
Source: Race and ethnicity data from superintendent's annual report, FY 2021.

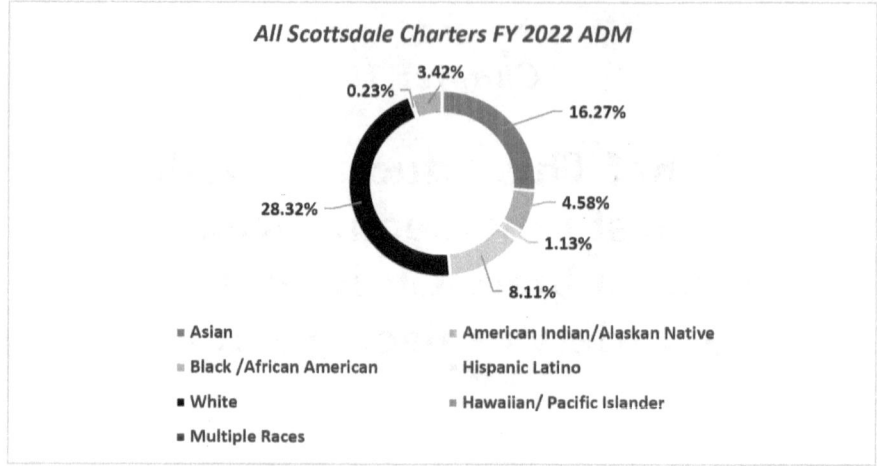

Figure 10.2. Race and Ethnicity at All Scottsdale Charters
Source: Race and ethnicity data from superintendent's annual report, FY 2021.

The macro data show that Asian children are vacating Scottsdale's public schools, with Latino students following suit.

MICRO DATA

Next, a closer look at the individual charter choices reveals how we are moving into an ethnically-segregated configuration. We are "schooling alone" by ethnicity and by choice.

Using the superintendent's annual report, an analysis shows where the special-needs students who either moved into the Scottsdale district or choose to attend a charter in Scottsdale went. The typical percentage of special education students in our nation's school systems is 9%.

To ensure we were considering poverty as a factor, percentages of free and reduced lunches are analyzed in Figure 10.5. The facts show that poorer students are prominent in the charter sector. This fact made us look at each school's ethnicity closer.

The figures in Chapter 10 are presented with little commentary regarding why people are choosing the schools they are choosing.

Individual Charter Schools in Scottsdale
Ethnicity Charts

In Figure 10.6, the newest BASIS School shows an even greater percentage of Asian and white students' parents choosing to attend BASIS, increasing

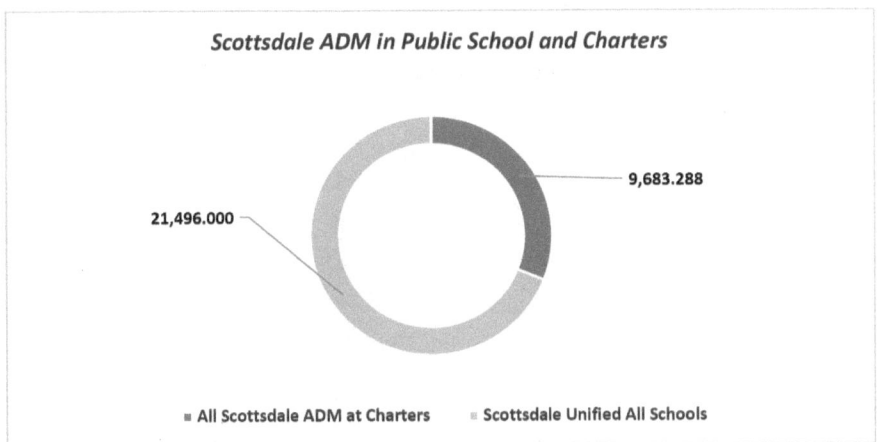

Figure 10.3. Total ADM FY 2021 Charter and Public Schools in Scottsdale
Source: Superintendent's annual report on race and ethnicity, FY 2020.

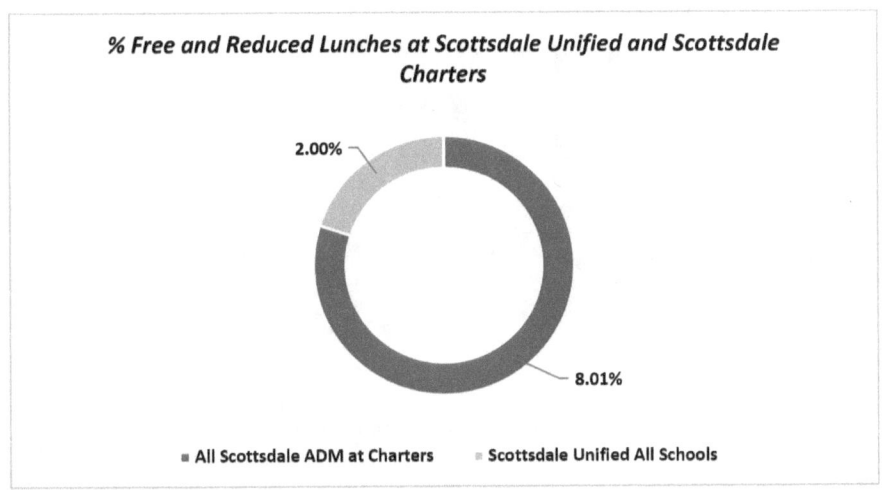

Figure 10.5. Percentages of Free and Reduced Lunch at Scottsdale Unified and All Scottsdale Charters, FY 2022
Source: Superintendent's annual report on race and ethnicity, FY 2020.

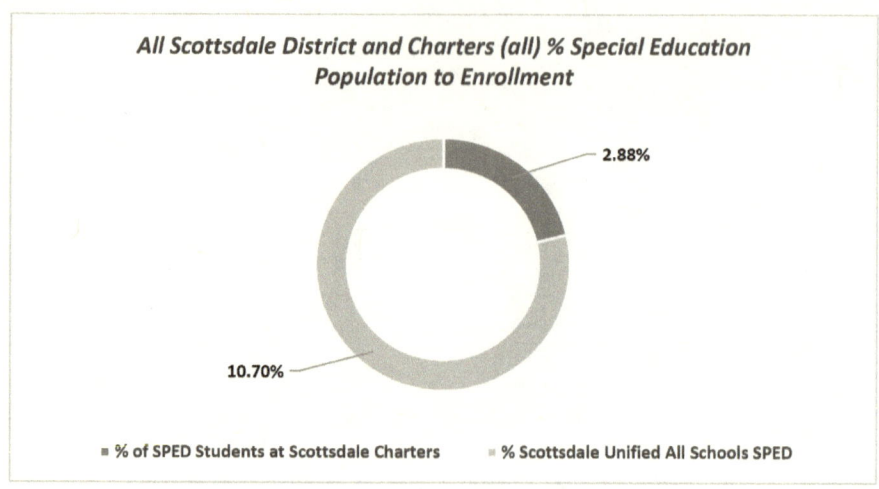

Figure 10.4. Special Education Students in Scottsdale, FY 2022
Source: Superintendent's annual report on race and ethnicity, FY 2020.

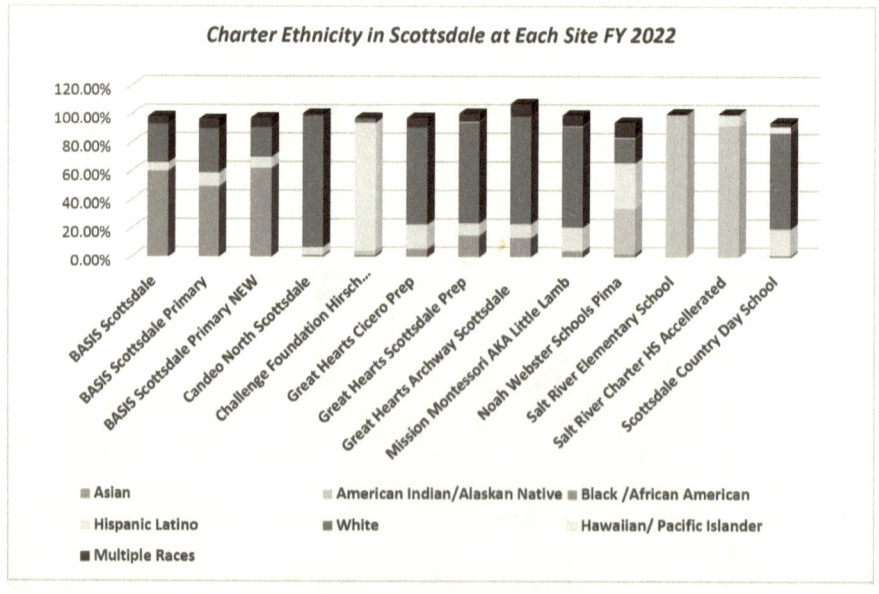

Figure 10.6. Ethnicity at Each Charter in Scottsdale, FY 2022
Source: Superintendent's annual report on race and ethnicity, FY 2020.

the chances that the BASIS School serving the older students will reflect a greater concentration than now exists.

PRIVATE SCHOOLS LOCATED IN SCOTTSDALE OR IN SURROUNDING TOWNS

State Scholarship Beneficiaries in High-Income Cities

The following analysis looks at the cities near Scottsdale, and it includes Paradise Valley and Fountain Hills. There were 63 private schools located in these cities. Paradise Valley and Scottsdale private schools had a total of $168 million in revenues from Arizona's scholarship programs.

It is anticipated that all students in these 63 private schools will apply for and receive voucher payments in FY 2024.

Horace Mann's hope was, "That this education will be best provided in schools that embrace children from a variety of backgrounds." One of the known factors in a child's success in any school is their mother's level of academic achievement (i.e., how far she went in school). Another key factor is the vocabulary and background information that a child brings to school. This vocabulary factor has been studied extensively, most notably through the work of Robert Marzano.[1] In 1987, Nagy and Coleman came up with an average vocabulary of 5,000 to 10,000 words for kindergarten.[2] The reality is that a large percentage of children enter school with a vocabulary of 3,500 words or less. In order to reach a goal of 50,000-word vocabularies by the end of high school, schools need to immerse children in a rich program of vocabulary enhancement of about 3,500 new words per year.

That goal is made easier when children with a low vocabulary are surrounded by children and adults with a wider vocabulary. Horace Mann knew this intuitively. One of the tragic parts of the movement to homeschool or use a micro-school approach is that many of those electing this path do not have the background or vocabulary to effectively counter this major blockage to comprehension.

Teachers and schools by themselves can't accomplish this goal. Students fall further and further behind when they don't know what the words they are saying mean. This means they need to have teachers who prepare them to read the topics in their texts by reviewing new vocabulary prior to reading a selection. Online classes that have these words highlighted and the definitions easily within reach may accomplish this, but there is little evidence that students who are struggling use these timely cues.

Competent teachers are intuitive when they are working with a student face-to-face. They can see the struggle in a child's face and react to it in real time. Artificial intelligence and sophisticated software that are supposed to mimic an expert teacher cannot replace this human interaction.

Our public schools have always taken all students as they are. They need the general public to understand that they are part of the "schooling alone" issue that is dividing us by social strata and ethnicity and is continuing to divide us politically.

You do have a choice. Choose wisely, and take responsibility for your choices. Our republic depends on it.

NOTES

1. https://www.marzanoresources.com/reproducibles/teaching-basic-advanced-academic-vocabulary
2. https://eric.ed.gov/?id=ED298471

Afterword

As this work was being put together, I intentionally placed several of my key points on social media hoping to obtain even greater insights into what the general public believes they know about Horace Mann's design for public common schools in our republic. At the same time, I probed for their understanding of the economic theories of action postulated by Milton Friedman and those advocating for using taxpayer resources to fund privately owned secular and nonsecular private schools.

One of the recurring thoughts and critiques of Horace Mann that needs further discussion is the idea that when he visited the Prussian and British school models (at his own expense), he adopted those models wholesale.

This theory of Mann's intent flies in the face of his original principles of education in a republic.

1. Citizens may not obtain both ignorance and freedom.
2. The public should have to pay for, control, and maintain education.
3. Children from different financial ladders should get the same education.
4. The education that is taught must be nonsectarian (nonreligious).
5. The education taught has to use tenets of a free society.
6. This education should be taught by professionally trained teachers.

Mann chose elements of the Prussian system that included the establishment of a graded elementary school program with children placed into grade levels. Identification of those who would go on to a higher level of publicly supported education was built into the Prussian model, as was a model to assist students going into the trades by learning from practicing tradesmen.

The Prussian model that was designed to produce "obedient" citizen soldiers was rejected by Horace Mann. Also rejected was the British and Prussian religious control of education in those countries—the same religions that are amply represented in the new "choice" schools supported by taxpayer funds for vouchers. Mann's continuous advocacy for schools free from corporal punishment and the humiliation of students put him at odds with the nascent teaching profession of the times he lived in.

Elements of these principles are embedded in many state constitutions, which puts those states in the precarious position of violating their own constitutions when they ignore Mann's second principle.

Plato's *Republic* speaks of philosopher kings ruling the republic (i.e., an educated class of rulers). Horace's democratic republic model of education is the antithesis of this model. This is evident in all of the principles he put forward.

The idea that public common schools were designed to keep the working class of our population obedient and willing to endure the factory models coming into being while Horace Mann was still alive is also a fallacy. "The education taught has to use the tenets of a free society" is a direct reproach to those who speak of "freedom to choose." That word "freedom" in Horace's first principle has been co-opted by those promoting the privatization of public education.

The ultimate goal of the push to privatize is the eventual demise of public education in our republic. During the Libertarian Party's 1972 presidential bid, this was their position on education:

> We support the repeal of all compulsory education laws, and an end to government operation, regulation, and subsidy of schools. We call for an immediate end of compulsory busing.

This is what the "conservative caucus" and its billionaire supporters would like to see become the future of education in our republic. The 1980 candidate for Libertarian vice president was David Koch. This followed his donation of $2 million into the party's coffers.

WHO CHOOSES, WHO LOSES?

The financing of private choices is underwritten by the junk bond industry and tax-free bonds issued by the IDA (Industrial Development Authority) at the state and county levels. The federal government has also pumped billions into efforts to replicate and support charter school expansion. If it weren't for ESSER funding and PPP loans during the pandemic years, the majority of charters would have lost money during that period. This despite the fact that their primary revenue sources had not dried up during the pandemic.

Voucher amounts are often half the cost of a private school tuition, which is often greater than the amount per student spent at an A-rated public school.

There is a reason why the "choice" industry has rejected the original charter model proposed by Ray Budde. Money. At last count, we collectively spend $794.7 billion on education in our republic. The ultimate goal is to place all of that money into corporate hands, even those funds raised at the local level, which is approximately half of the amount.

Efforts now afoot try to convince parents that homeschooling and micro-schools are an "affordable" way for parents to "have the freedom to choose," while private schools that keep charging more for tuition and use preferential selection processes for student selection are the wave of the future. This is a throwback to the days of "Dame Schools." Efforts to change child labor laws in "choice" states in order to make it possible to work while attending "homeschools" or micro-schools are not a coincidence.

The corporate takeover of public education funding is a benefit to the financial markets.

Consider when we were told that HMOs would benefit our health services by bringing a business model to the medical profession. How did that work out?

Benjamin Franklin's brief comment to the papers reporting on the Constitutional Convention is being ignored by those trying to convince the public to privatize our public common schools: "A republic, if you can keep it." The efforts to privatize play into a philosophical model represented by one of Milton Friedman's most-quoted statements regarding the social responsibility of a private corporation:

> The only social responsibility of business is to increase its profits.

Compare this to Horace Mann's challenge to graduates of Antioch College and our former normal schools:

> Be ashamed to die without winning some small victory for mankind.

Whose theory of education in a republic do we really believe in?

Schooling alone in separate educational "programs" continues to drive us apart from each other as we become "educated" by different, often conflicting models of education. The public is carefully kept ignorant of the fact that our money is now being spent on at least 14 different churches, sects, and religions that differ significantly in their version of the truth. Islamic law and the Koran; Lutheran, Baptist, Catholic, Congregationalist, and other sects with different versions of biblical laws; the Jewish Talmud; Hindu teachings from the Bhagavad Gita; Buddhism, Confucianism, and Taoism; atheism; and schools set up by sexual identity are not the way to bring us together as citizens of our republic.

Many of our charter choices boast of a "traditional" model of education. If traditional is such a wonderful "choice," then certainly the organizations that originally provided that tradition are up to the task. Public schools need to listen to the discontent with their current model and get back to the original intent of common schools. Dropping courses that teach civics and the Constitution are always a bad choice.

Our interdependence on each other as citizens of a republic depends on our commitment to one another to support our common schools. We have always had choices. What we have never had until now is government funding for those private and sectarian choices.

Index

Adams, John, 21
Adams, John Quincy, 67, 79
advertising, 20
African American, 13
ALEC, 29, 48, 83, 84, 128, 152
American Federation of Teachers, 71, 123
American Legislative Exchange Council, 29, 83, 152
Americans for Prosperity, 29
Anglican, 6, 29
antidiscrimination rules, 17
Antioch College, 12, 133
Arizona, 8, 9, 17, 21, 24, 29, 21, 24, 26, 34, 48, 73, 85, 87, 88, 89, 90, 91, 94, 96, 98, 99, 101, 114, 117, 120, 126, 140, 143, 144, 145, 152, 156, 163, 167, 171
artificial intelligence, 41, 168
asset ratio, 26, 33, 103, 104
autocratic, 29

backpacks full of cash, 30, 44, 141, 154
bailout, 9, 16, 75
bank failures, 16
Baptist, 23, 29, 24, 125, 131, 132
BASIS, 22, 48, 166
Beecher, Henry Ward, 66

birth control via educational cost decisions, 14
Block, Michael, 47
Block, Olga, 48
British public schools, 6, 57
Brown v. Board of Education, 1, 13, 14, 55, 73, 88, 139
Budde, Ray, 2, 70, 71, 72, 83, 110, 112, 122, 123, 171
bureaucratic, 3, 29, 95, 96

Calvinism, 80, 131
capital, 9
capitalism, 14, 19, 20, 37, 51, 69, 84, 150, 155, 160
Carson v. Makin, 27, 50
Catholic school, 6, 25, 56, 106, 120
Center for Educational Reform, 39, 60
Chambers of Commerce, 85
Channing, William Ellery, 65
charter corporations, 9, 97, 99, 111, 121
charter management group, 20
Chesterton, G. K., 5, 6
Child Find, 50
China, 20, 22, 23, 48
Chinese investors, 22
Christian, 19, 20, 21, 29, 24, 25, 26, 49, 88, 90, 105, 117, 118, 120, 123, 132, 135, 149

Church of England, 6, 29, 41, 63
ClassWallet, 22, 49, 101, 116
common education, 21, 22, 27, 30, 36, 39, 43, 52, 62, 69
common public schools, 8, 24, 58, 65
common schools, 5, 6, 8, 10, 13, 27, 28, 29, 32, 33, 34, 39, 40, 41, 42, 52, 69, 70, 81, 82
conservative, 5, 13, 17, 29, 36, 45, 48, 50, 53, 56, 81, 83, 124, 128, 139, 152, 155
conservatives, 1, 14, 36, 55, 84, 156
constitution (state), 15, 49, 51, 124, 131, 140, 156
construction, 9, 26, 157
Continental Congress, 23
corporal punishment, 68
corporate board, 10, 30, 73, 107
corporately owned, 19
Cremin, Lawrence A., 6, 82

Dame Schools, 6, 27, 70
Danbury Baptist Church, Connecticut, 23
debt, 9, 15, 26, 33, 74, 100, 102, 103, 104
Deists, 81, 132
democratic republic, 21, 45, 150
Department of Education, 26, 21, 27, 35, 36, 72, 97, 158, 171
Department of Health, Education, and Welfare, 35

economic social engineering, 14
economic theory, 14, 84, 151
Education Enterprise Zone Act, 84
educational choice, 15, 24, 92, 153, 155, 157, 158
educational funding, 16, 25, 43, 48, 120
elected governing board, 10
emancipation, 7
Emmons, Nathanael, 3, 80, 132, 133
English episcopal system, 42
entitlement, 22, 27, 29, 30, 37, 39, 43, 55, 77, 116, 145, 155, 156, 158, 160

equal employment opportunity, 27
equal opportunity, 22, 47
equalization formulas, 19, 40, 153
Espinoza v. Montana Department of Revenue, 50
ESSER, 9, 35, 53, 74, 98, 99, 145
establishment clause, 19, 116
eugenics, 14
Everson v. Board of Education, 25

Fair Labor Standards Act of 1938, 21
federal, 5, 8, 9, 15, 17, 26, 27, 25, 29, 31, 34, 35, 38, 40, 42, 43, 46, 49, 51, 53, 72, 74, 77, 83, 97, 98, 99, 100, 101, 102, 115, 125, 146, 147, 151, 156, 160, 171
federalism, 39, 53
First Amendment, 16, 20, 31, 127, 158
for profit, 24, 25, 20, 21, 32, 48, 73, 97, 101, 109
Forten, Charlotte, 12, 13
Forten, James, 13
founders, 21
Franklin, Massachusetts, 11, 21, 65, 79, 81, 82, 129, 130, 171
Franklin, Benjamin, 7, 30, 65, 79, 129, 149
Freedom Caucus, 72, 85
freedom of choice, 44
freedom of religion, 22, 23, 80, 159
freedom to choose, 5, 7, 9, 14, 28, 37, 38, 48, 51, 55, 56, 127, 150, 154, 155, 157
freemen, 12
Friedman, Milton, 2, 7, 13, 14, 29, 35, 36, 37, 38, 39, 40, 44, 45, 47, 53, 55, 69, 72, 83, 84, 88, 92, 95, 96, 104, 109, 126, 127, 135, 141, 151, 152, 156, 171
Friedman's Folly

gay, 21
Goldwater, Barry, 5, 8, 36, 38, 46, 84
Goldwater Institute, 47, 74, 158
governing board, 69, 73, 84

Index

Grand Canyon Institute, 18, 19, 34, 73, 87, 88, 89, 96, 98, 99, 102, 117, 118, 144, 145, 171

Hawthorne, Nathaniel, 65
Heritage Foundation, 27, 72
Hindu, 24
homeschooling, 6, 28, 152, 155
Horace's Hope, 2, 8, 10, 39, 41, 45, 52, 65, 171
Horne, Tom, 91

Industrial Development Authority, 9, 26, 30, 32, 100, 101
innovation and improvement, 97
Institute for Justice, 50
Institute for New Economic Thinking, 13
integration, 12, 127
intercept, 26, 32
interest-only payments, 15
Islamic, 29, 24, 88, 117

Jefferson, Thomas, 21 23, 25, 30, 31, 81, 116, 125, 149
Jewish, 29, 24, 25, 88, 118
Johnson, Andrew, 35
Johnson, Lyndon, 35, 48
junk bonds, 9, 32

Kirk, Charlie, 23
Koch, David, 29, 151
Koch brothers

land set-asides for public education, 22
LDS (Mormons), 20
LGBTQ, 26, 51
libertarian, 14, 15, 18, 29
Littky, Dennis, 71
lobbying groups, 20, 51
local control, 1, 5, 15, 19, 32, 34, 36, 46, 47, 56, 69, 71, 73, 84, 95, 146
Locke v. Davey, 49, 158
Lowell Public Schools, 20

MacLean, Nancy, 13, 29
Madison, James, 81
Maine, 17, 26, 50, 131
management costs, 96
Mann, Horace, 2, 5, 6, 12, 13, 21, 27, 28, 29, 41, 42, 51, 57, 59, 60, 62, 65, 66, 67, 68, 69, 77, 79, 80, 81, 82, 83, 92, 94, 106, 112, 114, 120, 124, 128, 129, 130, 131, 132, 133, 135, 137, 146, 149, 159, 167, 168
Mann, Stephen, 80, 133
market-based approach, 5
market education, 39, 44, 59, 60, 69, 88
Massachusetts Board of Education, 12, 57, 83, 128
mega-charters, 29
micro-schools, 6, 26, 27, 28, 147
ministers, 20, 24, 49, 120
ministers' salaries, 20
monopolies and price fixing, 20, 69
Monroe, James, 81
moral, 6, 21, 52, 67, 82, 85, 92, 140, 141
Mott, Lucrecia, 65
Muslim, 25

National Defense Education Act, 8, 35, 43
neighborhood effect, 39
neoconservatives, 15
"New Light" Calvinism, 80
New York City, 22
94-142, 27, 40
No Child Left Behind, 39, 40, 115
Nobel Learning, 22, 23
nonprofit, 24, 25, 21, 29, 73, 74, 75, 76, 101, 102, 108, 152
nonsectarian, 3, 5, 17, 18, 24, 25, 28, 27, 29, 43, 50, 68, 115, 117, 118, 128, 158, 160
normal school, 12, 13, 171
Northwest Ordinance, 22

Obama, Barack, 17, 75
online schools, 20

Oregon, 25, 27
overleveraged, 26
overseas equity funds, 21

Peabody, Mary, 65, 94, 129, 133, 135
Peabody sisters, 65, 133
Pearl Incident, 67
petitioned articles, 16
philosopher kings, 81
Pierce v. Society of Sisters, 25
plantation schools, 27
Plato's *Republic*, 81
Plessey v. Ferguson, 55
PPP, 9, 35, 53, 98, 99, 145
preschools and day care, 23
Primavera Capital Group, 23
private equity, 15, 26, 20, 21, 22
private schools, 6, 8, 9, 10, 15, 20, 22, 24, 25, 28, 19, 20, 21, 22, 25, 26, 28, 29, 32, 36, 47, 48, 51, 56, 59, 60, 72, 74, 75, 84, 88, 91, 92, 96, 100, 104, 112, 118, 126, 137, 142, 143, 145, 158, 167
projections, 15
property taxes, 24, 25, 28, 32, 35, 40, 75
public common education, 5, 10, 19, 67, 74, 81, 83
public common schools, 1, 7, 9, 10, 13, 25, 27, 19, 26, 28, 30, 33, 35, 40, 45, 52, 58, 60, 62, 71, 79, 82, 159, 160
public school choice grants, 72

Ravitch, Diane, 25
Reagan, Ronald, 5, 84, 146
real estate market crash, 15
related-party transactions, 20
religious sects, 28, 19, 32, 133
reproductive decisions, 14
republic, 1, 5, 6, 7, 10, 15, 19, 20, 21, 22, 27, 29, 19, 23, 25, 30, 38, 39, 41, 45, 49, 51, 52, 55, 58, 61, 62, 65, 67, 68, 69, 70, 77, 79, 80, 81, 82, 83, 84, 92, 125, 127, 128, 131, 137, 141, 145, 149, 150, 151, 152, 153, 155, 159

The Republic and the School, 6, 65, 82
right to bear arms, 31
Roe v. Wade, 55
Roger Williams the Creation of the American Soul, 80
Roosevelt, Franklin D., 21, 37, 81, 82

Salem Normal School, 13
Salem, Massachusetts, 12, 69
school boards, 15, 58, 74, 112, 121
school district meetings, 32, 58
Second Amendment, 14
sectarian, 17, 18, 21, 22, 24, 25, 28, 19, 24, 26, 27, 28, 32, 37, 43, 49, 50, 51, 80, 83, 86, 105, 107, 115, 116, 118, 119, 121, 124, 126, 128, 137, 140, 152, 153, 158, 159
separation clause, 17, 27
separation of church and state, 19, 22, 25, 125
Serrano v. Priest, 40
Shanker, Albert, 71, 123
slavery, 7, 22, 60, 69, 138
slaves, 7, 8, 13, 36, 37, 42, 70, 79
Spring Education Group, 22, 23
state constitutions, 10, 16, 49, 121
state-guaranteed loan programs, 26
STO, 18, 88, 119
Stowe, Harriet Beecher, 65
superintendent of public instruction, 26, 53, 91
supplement, not supplant, 42
supreme courts, 17
Symington, Fife, 48

Taft Bill, 25
tax exemption, 24
Tenth Amendment, 1, 14, 15, 16, 31, 116
territorial, 10
Thayer High School, 71, 171
Title I, 43, 98
Trinity Lutheran Church of Columbia v. Comer, 50
The Troubled Crusade, 25

Turning Point USA, 23, 141, 157

Underground Railroad, 67
underwater, 9
Unitarian, 80, 132, 133
universal voucher expansion, 17
University of Massachusetts at Salem, 13, 59, 123, 171
University of Massachusetts, Amherst, 70
U.S. Constitution, 14, 19, 22, 23, 31, 116, 125, 154
USDA, 9, 98
U.S. Supreme Court

voucher reimbursements to the parent, 26
vouchers, 8, 16, 17, 18, 23, 26, 27, 28, 34, 39, 42, 43, 44, 46, 49, 50, 56, 72, 77, 83, 84, 89, 101, 112, 115, 116, 117, 126, 127, 140, 142, 145, 146, 159

Wall Street investors, 26
Wall Street Journal, 22, 115
Whig Party, 67
white supremacy, 14
will of the people, 16, 43

About the Author

Curtis Cardine has been an educator since 1972 when he first entered the classroom as part of an experiment to involve young male teachers in a kindergarten classroom in Nahant, Massachusetts. In 1974 he sat in on presentations by Dr. Ray Budde as he discussed the potential for district-based charter schools. He graduated from Salem State College (formerly Salem Normal School, now the University of Massachusetts at Salem) in 1974 with an elementary education degree with a mathematics minor.

He competed as an Olympic weightlifter on multiple U.S. teams between 1974 and 1985. His teaching career included second, fifth, and sixth grade. At the same time, he filled in for high school and junior high mathematics and computer science classes at Thayer High School when there were teacher shortages in those areas. Simultaneously, Mr. Cardine ran multiple businesses. He is an expert on school and charter finances with multiple classes at the graduate level and beyond and guest lecturer positions on this topic at Antioch College. Mr. Cardine received a master's degree in organization and management from Antioch in 1987. He has been an adjunct professor at Franklin Pierce College and has run programs for aspiring principals at Keene State College and organization and management classes at Antioch.

He served as superintendent of schools from 1999 to 2005 in a multidistrict supervisory union in New Hampshire. During that time, he led a team that applied for and received a federal grant from the Department of Education to start district charter schools. That program was funded at $12.5 million for five years. When the program ended, several towns and one high school program converted to full charter programs. These programs still exist in New Hampshire.

In 2006 he became an educational leader at a hybrid charter school (online and in person) in Arizona and left that position to become a large charter group superintendent. After leaving that post, he became a researcher and consultant producing multiple papers for the Grand Canyon Institute (a nonpartisan organization).

He has written three books to date: *Carpetbagging America's Public Schools*; *Schooling Alone*; and *Horace's Hope, Friedman's Folly*.

www.ingramcontent.com/pod-product-compliance
Lightning Source LLC
Chambersburg PA
CBHW030143240426
43672CB00005B/252